ON THE MONEY JOURNAL

C. Stephen Guyer's guide for how you can acquire, borrow, protect, move, watch, play with, go to jail for, and have fun with, our most popular commodity—

Money!

C. Stephen Guyer

Parsifal Press

Highlands Ranch, Colorado

Published by Parsifal Press, an imprint of GMA, Inc., Highlands Ranch, Colorado. To contact the publisher, write to:

John Eschenbach
Parsifal Press
1708 Grizzly Gulch Ct
Highlands Ranch, CO 80129
Telephone: (303) 683-3338
Email: pr@guyermanagement.com

ISBN: 978-0-9779405-0-9

Printed in the United States of America

Editorial team leader: Ruth E. Smith

Dedicated to the memory of:

John Paul William Beard

CONTENTS

Preface

On the Money—now in its fifth year of syndication—is the financial column C-level executives just can't wait to get their hands on. Published monthly by American Cities Business Journals, *On the Money* is a refreshingly candid (and sometimes humorous) look at the stuff that makes the world go 'round.

Now, for the first time, a compilation of C. Stephen Guyer's favorite columns is available in ***On the Money Journal***: Guyer's guide for how you can acquire, borrow, protect, move, watch, play with, go to jail for, and have fun with, our most popular commodity—Money!

ACQUIRING NEW MONEY

Business is the art of extracting money from another man's pocket without resorting to violence.

- Max Amsterdam

A good business plan should spell out the bottom line

Ralph Waldo Emerson said, "Build a better mousetrap and the world will beat a path to your door." That tenet may still ring true, but will anyone pay for it?

In financial circles, it's not about the mouse or the trap; it's about the money.

When raising money, the basic questions "How much? What are you going to do with it? What do the investors get in return?" must be stated within the first 100 words of any business plan proposal for funding.

Imagine attending a concert where the orchestra is seated and ready to play. The conductor walks onto the stage and launches into a soliloquy on the nature of compositional techniques, the relative worth of this piece as it applies to the vast human aesthetic experience, the subtleties of the acoustics in this particular hall, what everyone in the orchestra is wearing and planning to do after the concert, various alternative forms of transportation to get the audience home after the concert, a tabular statistical summary of child-care alternatives employed by those in attendance—and never plays a note of music!

That's what it's like for the financial person who reads a business plan that excludes those key 100 words.

It may sound simple and a little disheartening to the entrepreneur, but without these simple essentials stated right away, no one will read the plan.

Breaking down the critical 100 words looks like this:

- **How much?** Start with one number summarized from cash-flow projections. It should be the amount of money needed over the next three years to carry out the development and expansion of the business. Set this stage quickly to avoid any waste of time. Many investors have specific parameters for how much or how little they are willing to consider.

If you have sophisticated financial help, also indicate the proportion of funds that will come from the sale of stock and bank borrowing. Describe the kind (common stock, convertible debenture, etc.), unit price and total amount of securities to be sold.

• **What are you going to do with it?** For a new business, the cash-flow forecast is more important than any other prediction because it details the amount and timing of expected cash inflows and outflows. This is where the use of the new funds is shown.

Usually the level of net income is insufficient to finance operating cash needs. Moreover, cash inflows never match the outflows on a short-term basis. The cash-flow forecast clarifies these conditions.

Investors want to see specifically where their money is going. They do not want to see the new money replace old debt or liabilities, or give the owners above-average salaries, or pay for dog-and-pony road trip shows that will only raise more money, thereby diluting their position. Show on the cash-flow statement that this money will operationally grow the business.

Given a level of projected sales and capital expenditures over a specific period, the cash-flow forecast highlights the need and timing of additional financing and shows peak requirements of working capital.

You also may show how this additional financing will be obtained, on what terms, and how it is to be repaid. Part of the needed financing may be supplied by the professional venture capitalists, part by bank loans of one to five years, and the balance by short-term lines of credit. All of this information becomes part of the final cash-flow forecast.

- **What does the investor get in return?** This raises the thorny issue of company valuation. A basic bare-bones rate of return is "what you got" divided by "what you gave." An additional wrinkle is whether the "got" part of the equation is cash or some other form of asset. You can work a relatively simple equation for this information: Multiply yearly revenue at the end of the third year by 1.5; multiply that by the equity percent held by the investor; divide that by the amount of cash given at the beginning.

This is a very basic return for investment calculation. It is astounding how many business plans neglect to provide even this fundamental inkling of potential return to the potential investor. Analysis that is more sophisticated can be, and probably will be, performed for each potential investor on a case-by-case basis that would also include issues relating to cash, debt vs. equity, preferential payment schedules, dilution and the like.

You probably do have a better mousetrap. Now, use your straight-shooting business plan to get the capital to make your company successful.

(March 2002)

When it comes to financing, cash flow still rules the roost

While the markets often focus on items such as net income, total assets, earnings per share, net worth, PE ratio, etc., the fact is this: You can't spend any of those things. You can, however, spend cash—arguably the most important measure of immediate value.

Unfortunately, the "Consolidated Statement of Cash-flows" is the last document in a presentation of "Standard Financial Statements." First is the Balance Sheet (primarily a measure of assets), then the Income Statement (mainly a presentation of earnings), and after that, almost as an afterthought, is the Cash-Flow statement. By the time most readers digest the first two presentations, there's hardly space for the beleaguered Statement of Cash-Flows. Nevertheless, this statement is the most valuable component of the financials. Why? Because cash is cash—you can spend cash.

Since our society has evolved to the point where we use "fiat money" rather than actual merchandise in our transactions, cash is the medium by which we convert and conduct all our business. ("Fiat money" is money the government declares is legal tender, rather than something of intrinsic value such as chickens, firewood, etc.) By contrast, if we still lived in a commodities-based culture such as farming, for example, we might create a report called the Statement of Cow-Flows.

For the investor, the Statement of Cash-Flows is the place to start when looking for insights into the management of an enterprise. Aside from the obvious measure of how much cash is on hand, the statement shows where the currency came from and where it went. The Statement of Cash-Flows provides three major categories for presentation. They are: cash provided by or (used) from 1) operating activities, 2) investing activities, and 3) financing activities.

The first thing to observe on a Statement of Cash-Flows is the proportion of cash provided by each of the three areas mentioned above. The mixture provides an indication of the company's maturity, focus, strength and emphasis. A company whose main source of cash is not from operations may be new, in transition, in trouble, heavily involved in ancillary activities or any combination thereof.

The reason there is such a need for cash-flow analysis is due to something called "accrual" accounting. Under the accrual method of accounting, a company may recognize revenue as soon as there is an event that creates an obligation on the part of the customer to pay. The same is true for expenses documented by the company when it has an obligation to pay a supplier. Revenue does not mean cash was received. Expense does not mean cash was paid out. There is a vast difference between revenue from operating activities and cash from operating activities. You can't spend revenue.

An example of accrual accounting is, I "sell" you a glass of lemonade on a hot day; you give me a smile and promise to pay me in a week. I gave you the product, you promised to pay me, but I have no cash. Therefore, I earned some revenue but received no fiat money for my goods.

Within the category of "cash from operating activities," there are several things the potential investor will want to note, including:

- **Gains or losses from the sale of assets.** Is the company inflating net income through the sale of assets, rather than sound operating activities?

- **Gains or losses from the sale of investments.** The investor should ascertain what the investments were in the first place and why they were sold.
- **Cash provided or used by certain changes in receivables, payables, prepaid expenses, and inventory.** If the amounts for receivables and payables are not substantially the same, there may be a collection problem. If payables are increasing, there may be an underlying cash crunch or a brewing dispute with a supplier. Excessive inventory buildup or depletion may be discovered here as well.

A basic sign of a mature, vigorous company is that cash from operations is greater than net income. If that's not the case, then the prospective investor must look deeper to discover what's really going on. Many times it means that the firm is new and still raising capital or investing in plant and equipment. However, the perceptive investor will know this by analysis, not assumption.

Within the "cash from investing and financing activities," notable items to watch for are:

- **Capital expenditures.** Is the company investing in itself? The type of purchases should be revealed in the "notes to the financial statements."
- **Dividends paid.** Watch for trend fluctuations. If there is a jump from previous periods, ask why.
- **Issuance or repurchase of stock.** Did the company recently issue a significant amount of stock? What will this do to your current or contemplated holdings? Any large amounts reported as "certain other" deserve special investigative attention.

Amid ever-increasing uncertainty and distrust of financial reporting, one statement remains readily available as a window into the real dealings of a firm. The next time you pick up an annual report, read the

Statement of Cash Flows first. Because at the end of the day, cash is what you, want. Why? Because cash is cash— you can spend cash.

(May 2002)

Why private placement financing is making a comeback

One of the most straight-forward resources for obtaining capital for a small business is also one of the oldest: private placement financing.

One example of private-placement financing is this true story: A fellow was enjoying a cigar at Churchill's Lounge at the Brown Palace Hotel. Three gentlemen, also smoking cigars, were discussing the oil business.

The first man, who was in a related business, overheard their conversation. He walked over to the group of three and said, "Here's what I'm up to," so they reached in their pocket and handed him $200,000. He wrote them an IOU on a napkin.

Simply put, private placement financing issues security directly to an investor and secures capital for the business owner without the banking industry's intermediation.

Though it's not always as serendipitous as the Churchill's Lounge example, private or informal investors are now, more than ever, searching for exceptional small business investment opportunities.

Despite the sluggish economy, I've run into more people with "funds on the side" in the past month than I have in my entire career.

Professor William E. Wetzel of the University of New Hampshire says informal investors represent the largest pool of risk capital in the country, financing 20,000 or more ventures per year.

Time was before small-business loans, venture capitalists and other banking-industry funding options, all deals were private placements.

Those who held excess funds sat face-to-face with those who needed them and agreements were made. To the chagrin of the banking industry, those good old days of straight-shot deals are back.

Furthermore, remove banking-industry underwriting or brokerage fees from the equation, and face-to-face financing is not just simple, it's economical.

Private placements come in three basic forms:

- Equity investment where the investor is given partial ownership of the venture;
- Debt investment where the investor is given a secured promissory note;
- Limited partnership or corporation.

Of these options, the limited partnership is most commonly used for transactions between $500,000 and $1 million. For the investor, limited partnerships serve two purposes:

They allow investors to assume limited liability. Creditors cannot look to the personal assets of the limited partners to satisfy partnership debts; the general partner assumes this risk, and losses for the limited partners are limited to the investment. All gains and losses from the venture flow directly to the partners; allowing the investor to report the gains and losses of the limited partnership on a personal tax return.

How does the small-business owner locate and secure private investors? Recent research profiles what a typical private placement investor might look like: 47 years-old, graduate degree, management experience with new ventures, likely to invest $20,000 to $50,000 in any one venture, participates in a private placement about once every two years, participates with other financially sophisticated individuals, invests within 50 to 300 miles of home, expects to liquidate the investment in five to 10 years, expects annual rates of return of 20 percent to 50 percent, depending on risk, learns of opportunities through friends and business associates, and is concerned with the "psychic income" from the venture, such as industry recognition.

A few sources for uncovering individuals with the means and desire to invest in a $500,000 to $1 million transaction include: CPAs who specialize in tax matters or focus on smaller privately held companies; attorneys who specialize in estate planning, tax strategies, and bankruptcy; commercial bankers, particularly those in "special assets" departments; venture capitalists who specialize in smaller startup and second stage financing; small-business owners who have an older, established client base; and chief financial officers of large corporations with self-funded pension and retirement plans.

A written partnership agreement helps clarify the particulars of the deal. In this agreement, items such as allocations of net income, net losses, credits, and distributions are specified.

The agreement usually describes eventualities such as liquidation, sale of partnership interests, apportionment, timing of distributions, liabilities, and tax considerations.

Ultimately, the small-business owner seeking financing knows that there's no substitute for sound business, financial and legal knowledge and seeks-out the same, thereby ensuring that all parties understand the nature of the risks involved.

(February 2002)

The VCs have awakened: What to do about it

After a dreary and depressing period of timidity and retreat, venture capitalists seem to be awakening.

They remained on a steady pace in the first quarter of 2006, investing $5.6 billion in 761 deals, according to PricewaterhouseCoopers. The quarter's dollar value matches the investment level from fourth quarter 2005 and represents a 12 percent increase over the same period last year.

According to Michael V. Copeland at *CNNMoney*, "There's never been a better time to start your own company. New technologies are creating new business opportunities on the Internet, on mobile phones, in consumer products and in information services."

According to Copeland, in the late 1990s, a typical VC-funded startup needed roughly $10 million to amass the infrastructure and staff required to carry the company from its first business plan to its first product launch. Today, the cost has been reduced to just $4 million. The barriers to entry never have been lower.

The combination of increased venture funding and a lower cost to market makes it a good time to review the essential elements for obtaining your share of this year's VC money. Here's the path.

An obvious first step is the business plan—which often is overlooked or underdeveloped. Remember these key points for superior business plan construction:

- Clearly and immediately show that the plan contains the basic components: company, product or service, customers, market, competition, and potential risk.

- The executive summary, no more than two pages, should simply answer these three questions:
  1. How much money do you want?
  2. What are you going to do with the money?
  3. How much will the investor receive in return?

- Make the purpose of your business obvious. Demonstrate that your personal skills and management team's experience are directly applicable to this opportunity.

- Explain how you will manufacture the product or provide the service—especially the source of your profit.

- Discuss general trends in your market and industry. Then, surgically identify the segment and the unfilled need. Demographics of your potential customers are useful, particularly if they strike a chord with the VC investors.

- Depict your competition in detail and the reasons for your superiority.

- Describe your marketing plan—the "4 P's" of price, place, promotion, and product.

- Prepare complete pro forma financial statements: balance sheet, income statement, cash-flow statement, and sources and uses of funds. The most important is cash flow.

Once the business plan is completed, the hardest part is gaining entry to the venture capital firm. In about 60 minutes, you must show why your business could be the best thing since peanut butter. Obviously, your presentation should be interesting, informative, and well-prepared.

Here are some specific insights for success:

- Conduct your own due diligence on the venture firm prior to the meeting. Know its focus, philosophy, successes, and failures.

- Prepare a set of questions you want to ask during your meeting. The best venture firms view their relationships as authentic partnerships—and that's what an entrepreneur should expect as well.
- Don't become lost in high-level market statistics. Focus on the essentials of what you are going to accomplish with the capital requested.
- Practice the entire presentation and time each section. Maintain control of the presentation's flow and don't wander. However, be prepared to digress if requested. By knowing the timing of each section, you'll be able to re-engage the presentation and still cover all critical parts.
- Have crucial documents (with enough copies for all) ready for review, such as the detailed pro forma financials, a customer reference list, and a current capitalization chart. Don't hand them out until the end of the presentation.
- Have backup plans in case of audiovisual failures and connectivity troubles for live Internet demonstrations.
- Be prepared for uncomfortable questions. Often, venture partners will ask bold questions about areas of concern. Address those questions immediately and then return to the overall presentation, tailoring the conclusion from those questions.
- Maintain a positive "risk-to-IPO" ratio. That is, the number of times you mention "risks" to the number of times you mention "IPO." Be forthright about the risks inherent in your business.
- If the presentation goes exceedingly well, have your company's bank wiring instructions ready. Include this information on the last slide of your presentation.

- If the presentation is heading south in a hurry, don't worry. Relax and have fun. A sense of humor is always helpful.

Remember the words of J. Paul Getty: "If you can count your money, you don't have a billion dollars."

(June 2006)

BORROWING SOMEONE ELSE'S MONEY

Credit is a system whereby a person who can not pay gets another person who can not pay to guarantee that he can pay.

- Charles Dickens

Creative Collateral

If you've ever applied for a loan, you've no doubt heard the term "collateral." During the early stages of a business needing capital, the word "collateral" may have been uttered so many times that the very sound of those syllables causes gastric distress. Lack of traditional collateral may force the frustrated borrower to think back to the old Bob Dylan song, "But I went into a bank, to get some bail for Arab, and all the boys back in the tank. They asked me for some collateral, and I pulled down my pants!"

Collateral is an asset pledged to a lender until a loan is repaid. If the loan is not repaid, the lender may seize the collateral and sell it to pay off the loan. (This makes the Dylan song even more fun to think about— but hardly practical in the banking biz.) Obvious forms of collateral include houses, cars, stocks, bonds, and cash; all things that are readily convertible into cash to repay the loan. Some of those assets are "hard," such as houses and automobiles; others are "paper," such as the stocks and bonds. That difference is important because of the amount of effort necessary for the lender to liquidate the asset. Lenders like assets that are easy and inexpensive to liquidate. Keep in mind that the collateral's worth is not based on the market value. It is discounted, taking into account the value that would be lost if the assets had to be liquidated quickly. However, there are other forms of collateral assets that are sometimes overlooked that can assist the new business in obtaining operating funds.

An asset is defined to be *anything* that has commercial or *exchange* value that is owned by a business, institution or individual. While exploring some of these less traditional forms of collateral, remember that you need a lender familiar with non-traditional lending. Federal and state chartered banks are constrained by regulations that strictly define collateral acceptance. Also, the riskier the collateral, and the more difficult it is to liquidate, the more expensive the loan.

In additional to intrinsic or "hard" value, anything that has revenue or a potential future earnings stream can be used as collateral. This includes contracts for purchase or purchase orders. A purchase order issued to you from one of your customers represents future sales on your part. The purchase order can then be used to secure a loan for cash today, "collateralized" by the promise of future payment by your customer.

Another form of collateral is loans you have either made to other people, simple accounts receivable, or formalized promissory notes. Those payments to you represent a revenue stream. It is possible to pledge the loans you hold as collateral for another loan to yourself. This goes on frequently on a larger scale of in the form of "collateral backed bonds" traded on Wall Street.

Often overlooked as a source of collateral is "future earning power." Basic to a lender's willingness to make a loan is an assessment of the future earning power of the organization or individual. To the extent that earning power is enhanced, the lender will look more favorably at the borrower. This is the principle behind all manner of educational loans; that is, with more education and training, the earning power of the borrower will be enhanced. However, universities and colleges are not the only organizations that increase earning power. There are lenders who specialize in more specific forms of training, such as: truck driving or bartending schools, medical procedures, commercial "learning centers," seminars, and even dating services. (Children are still not acceptable in most cases.)

In the very imaginative category, other items that have been used as collateral include: watches, jewelry, interests in box seats at a sports arena, golf club memberships, lawn mowers, suits of armor, opera tickets, antique furniture, art collections, vinyl record collections, insurance policies, medical instruments, lottery tickets, wine collections, tires, and even specialized pumpkin seeds.

The *Atlanta Business Chronicle* reports that at a time when recent Federal Reserve statistics show that 45 percent of domestic banks have tightened lending standards for small businesses, some non-traditional lenders such as the financial services division of brokerage houses have doubled its loan volume in the Atlanta area.

As the economy struggles out of its current distressed state, both lenders and borrowers are searching for more creative and non-traditional ways of facilitating cash flow. This means an increased willingness on the part of lenders to look at non-traditional collateral. It also means that borrowers should be open-minded and probing about what they may be willing to pledge.

(June 2005)

Arbitration rules not always fair when borrowing money

Many individuals and small businesses borrow money in times of crisis. The old saying, "If you don't need it, I'll lend it," seems particularly true. When we have excess money, usually we're not thinking of borrowing.

That situation opens the door for a subtle and dangerous form of lender protection called "mandatory binding arbitration" ("MBA"). Here's a closer look at this treacherous lending practice.

Binding arbitration clauses are often found in credit card agreements, automobile financing contracts, and many mortgage loans. The two largest arbitration companies are the National Arbitration Forum and the American Arbitration Association.

According to the National Consumer Law Center, the kind of passive notice that locks consumers into arbitration increasingly ties them to a system (privately funded with no connection to the courts) that thoroughly stacks the deck when serious disputes arise. Lenders alone select the arbitration service—often one dependent on them for repeat business.

Those same companies often write the arbitration rules. Not surprisingly, those rules often demand complete secrecy about the proceeding and its outcome while limiting what evidence consumers can present.

Consumers usually pay more for arbitration proceedings than they would for a public court proceeding. If they lose, there's no appeal. That means even legal errors in an arbitrator's decision are frequently beyond remedy. Moreover, if they refuse to participate in this rigged game, these clauses often dictate they'll automatically lose the dispute with no further recourse.

Here are problems and dangers.

- Arbitration frequently costs more than taking a case to court. In many cases, a borrower may have to pay a large fee simply to initiate or respond to the arbitration process. This can deter a borrower from even bringing a complaint. On a small claim, total fees for arbitration can easily exceed the amount awarded.

- Mandatory binding arbitration clauses generally bind only the borrower—not the lender. The lender retains its rights to take any complaint to court while the borrower can only initiate arbitration.

- Borrowers often are unaware they've agreed to binding arbitration. The mandatory binding arbitration clause is often tucked away in a paragraph of fine print or provided as a separate form. Lenders often don't mention it until the borrower is ready to sign the agreement.

- Credit card companies often issue a new card-member agreement, which by default must be accepted. These tactics deprive borrowers of their right to make an informed decision and create unconscionable contracts.

- Arbitration doesn't follow clear, well-established, consistent rules and procedures such as those required for litigation in the court system.

For example, arbitrators aren't required to follow procedures that enable one side in a dispute to request information from the other (legal "discovery"). The result is that borrowers, who usually have limited resources, have difficulty getting information needed to support their claims.

In addition, arbitrators aren't required to consider legal precedent in making their decisions. Most decisions can't be appealed, and there are generally no review bodies or other oversight to ensure that arbitrators follow fair procedure or the law.

- The lender generally picks the arbitration company.

In theory, both parties agree to the selection of a neutral, independent arbitrator. In reality, the lender designates the arbitration company in the contract. This situation can definitely affect the impartiality of the arbitrator.

As the above demonstrates, in mandatory binding arbitration, a lender requires a borrower to agree to submit any dispute that may arise to binding arbitration prior to completing a transaction with the company. The borrower is required to waive their right to sue, to participate in a class-action lawsuit, or to appeal.

The link between arbitration and legal enforceability is based on contract law. The arbitration decision is effectively a new contract between the parties.

Therein lies the hazard. The borrower has given up their full rights under the law. Furthermore, since the borrower was likely operating under the duress of a financial predicament, the bargaining positions of the lender and borrower weren't equal. This is the Doctrine of Duress and Unconscionability.

The concept of unconscionability has two elements: procedural unconscionability and substantive unconscionability

A contract is procedurally unconscionable when a party can't negotiate the terms of a contract because of unequal bargaining power or lack of meaningful choice. In addition, a contract may be procedurally unconscionable when terms are hidden within a contract.

A contract is substantively unconscionable when it imposes unduly harsh or oppressive, one-sided terms.

Courts have, and will refuse to enforce, a contract that is both procedurally and substantively unconscionable.

For more information regarding opposition to binding arbitration, visit:

www.stopbma.org,
www.consumersunion.org,
www.consumerlaw.org.

(August 2005)

The real cost of a loan often is hidden in the details

To paraphrase a famous nursery rhythm; "This little piggy went to market, this little piggy stayed home, this little piggy had roast beef, this little piggy had none, and THIS little piggy went wee, wee, wee—all the way to the bank!"

The last piggy worked for the pig that "had roast beef" who lent to the piggy that "had none." And that little piggy had made an 89 percent annualized return on her money, even though the interest rate was "only" 10.5 percent per year.

How did this happen? Let's dissect the transaction and discover how the real cost of a loan (and the genuine profit to the lender) is not always what it might seem.

From the borrower's perspective, the essential calculation for cost-of-money is based upon how much <u>cash</u> changed hands—not annual interest rate, accrued expenses, opportunity cost, amortized liability, or any other finance-industry term. In plain English, how much <u>cash</u> did you get for how much you gave back to the little piggy-- oops, lender?

Let's take a $100 example. You have no roast beef and wish to borrow $100 for one year. You find the little piggy with the beef and strike a deal. "You're a risky looking pig," says the beef-keeper. "The interest rate will be 10.5 percent per year."

Not exactly "prime," but nevertheless you agree. You start listing the costs associated with this loan, beginning with $10.50 interest costs.

Also, you get to pay an "origination fee." This is a fee (read up-front profit to the lender), for instigating this loan, even though you approached the lender. Origination fee: 3 percent, or $3.00. Instead of getting $100, you only receive $97.

Other items that appear in the form of fees that add to the real cost of funds by reducing the amount of <u>cash</u> you will receive include:

Original Issue Discount – Another creative term that represents nothing but additional return to the lender; in our example another 2 percent or $2.00.

Processing fee – You get to pay for the lender's secretarial and administrative support.

Filing fee – Once again, this item is a way for the lender to pass on their cost of doing business to you.

Account servicing fee – This is the lender's cost of keeping track of you and your payments. These three fees, for example, are $10.

Note: If you can imagine ANY possible fee, the lender may attach it. Examples include: EPA Report Costs, Closing Fees, and Document Preparations, just to name a few. For our discussion, let's say these fees add up to $5

In most cases the fees mentioned above are deducted from what you will receive as "loan proceeds," the cash you obtain. However, application fees are usually accepted up-front. You have the privilege of giving some of what you want to the person who already has it. In our example, let's use $5.

Pre-payment, which can be tricky, must be dealt with. In our example, the lender is expecting to receive 10.5% interest at the end of one year. Logic says that if you can repay your loan early, do so. However, there may be a pre-payment penalty. Sometimes the "penalty" is stated as a percent of the balance at the time of the pre-payment. In other situations, it can be hidden within amortization schedules.

The lender may present one amortization schedule for regular payments, but if the loan is pre-paid, another schedule is used so that the lender will still receive the same dollar amount of interest as if they had been at risk the entire time.

Let's assume the loan is paid off at 6 months but due to either a pre-payment penalty or double amortization schedule the lender still gets the full 10.5% ($10.50) even though the money was only at risk for half of that time.

Let's conduct a tally. The piggy with the beef gave the one with none $80.00— that's $100 less $3 origination fee, $2 original issue discount, $10 original issue, processing and filing fee, and $5 other fees. After 6 months, the lender receives $115.50— $100 principal, $10.50 in interest and the $5 application fee. On a cash basis, the profit is $115.50 minus $80 equaling $35.50. That's a 44.4% return on the cash money. And, since the loan was paid in only 6 months, the annualized return is 88.8 percent!

Generally, it is illegal to realize more than 45% profit from lending. If the profit is more than 45 percent, it's called usury—an area that is complex and filled with legal subtleties.

Nevertheless, when borrowing money, take a moment to conduct a cash-on-cash analysis to determine the authentic cost of the loan.

(December 2002)

Uncovering the mysteries of commercial banking

There are over 100 distinct commercial banks in the Denver metropolitan area, not counting branches or automated facilities. Even though many view banks as some omnipotent and mysterious source of all funds, small business owners often turn to banks as the first potential source of new money. What all banks have in common is their simplicity: they are merely balance sheets upon which appear their assets and liabilities. Savvy small business owners should want their companies on that list of assets. Small businesses that use traditional commercial bank financing are in fact an asset of that bank.

Persuading your banker of the worth of that asset can be a frustrating and baffling process. Cultivating relationships with bankers, speaking their language, and understanding the process of loan negotiation are critical elements of successful small business ownership.

Smart small business owners will acquire access to all of the commercial banks in their area, and then analyze each one. Minimally, the analyses should include these critical ratios: 1) Loans to Deposits, 2) Liquidity Ratio, and 3) Capital Ratio. These ratios provide an indication of the bank's receptiveness to making new loans. Further, understanding the ratios will help develop an approach that is consistent with the bank's current financial condition and temperament.

Loans-to-Deposits Ratio

This ratio is calculated by dividing loans by deposits. The average for most banks is 75 percent. The lower this ratio, the more conservative the bank's attitude generally is toward lending.

Liquidity Ratio

The liquidity ratio is calculated by adding cash, federal funds sold, U.S. government securities, and 70 percent of state and municipal securities. This sum yields the bank's total liquid assets. To determine the liquidity ratio, divide liquid assets by total deposits. A representative (Denver) commercial bank has a liquidity ratio of about 35 percent. Typically, the lower this ratio, the more aggressive the bank's position toward making new loans (i.e., the more likely the bank is to lend money).

Capital Ratio

The capital ratio is determined by dividing the sum of capital, surplus, and undivided profits by the total deposits. This ratio is often between 5 and 7 percent, and the representative (Denver) bank has a capital ratio of 8 percent. The lower this ratio, the more aggressive and therefore the more receptive the bank may be toward lending.

Although these three ratios provide a general indication of the bank's relative conservatism or aggressiveness, other components should be considered as well—most of them available in the bank's annual report.

The chairman's opening letter in the bank's annual report, for example, is often a particularly revealing indication of the bank's lending posture. In narrative form, the message presents the bank's overall results of the past year and, more importantly, outlines the bank's position and strategies for the future. Keep in mind that these letters are written for shareholders; attempting to keep that group comfortable with the bank's intentions.

A more detailed and insightful analysis may be performed using information found in the bank's

Supplemental Schedules and Notes to the Financial Statements.

Items that should be monitored and analyzed include:

Allowance for Loan Losses- a measure of the institution's pessimism or optimism.

Loan Analysis by Category- commercial, construction, real estate, installment, etc.

Off Balance Sheet Financial Instruments- may be a measure of responsiveness and flexibility. Recently however, this could also be an enormous warning signal that will require additional analysis.

Legal Proceedings- not always bad, as it may indicate the protection of assets.

Problem Assets- many real estate loans of the mid-1990s may be found here, also many failed telecommunication companies. (Do you need some cheap routers?)

Loan Concentration by Industry- usually containing a category for commercial real estate along with manufacturing, high technology, etc.

Loan Concentration by Collateral Type- often contains real estate types (construction, land, etc.) The most important is the distinction between "hard" and "paper" assets.

Foreclosed Real Estate- gives an indication of the bank's history with real estate lending and their aggressiveness in collections.

Loan Loss Experience- an indication of experience and therefore a measurement of willingness to lend in a particular area.

Using a database to store and access data on multiple banks, small business owners create access to powerful information that will help determine which institutions are likely to be the most receptive to their individual needs. For example, a small business owner might request a list of banks with loans-to-deposits greater than 70 percent, a declining loan loss experience in undeveloped land, and less than 30 percent of their loans in commercial real estate. The resulting register of institutions provides a solid starting point for the small business to obtain financing.

Identifying a bank based solely on financial or statistical information is just the beginning. Behind and within every organization, including banks, people make the decisions. Knowing and developing a genuine rapport with the parties of the transaction greatly improve the probability of success— for you as well as for the banker.

(April 2002)

Leveraged deals can financially benefit companies

The ancient Greek Archimedes said, "Give me a lever that is long enough, give me a fulcrum that is strong enough and give me a place to stand and single-handed I'll move the world."

He was describing the physics of "leverage."

In finance, leverage is borrowed money. To the extent assets are controlled by borrowed money, that's financial leverage.

Several years ago, the term Leveraged Buyout, ("LBO"), was frequently used in connection with acquisitions. Companies would buy control of another company (hopefully an asset), using borrowed funds. If the leverage was positive, the increase in value of the asset would be greater than the cost of the borrowed funds and the acquiring entity's return would be amplified.

For example, a manufacturing firm is considering purchasing a new machine for $250,000. The new machine will produce a new line of goods that the company believes will generate a profit of $75,000. If the firm has $250,000 of cash available, purchases the machine with the cash (100% equity, no leverage), the return on equity will be 30%. That is, a $75,000 return divided by the $250,000 cash investment.

Using financial leverage, the firm's banker offers to provide a $125,000 loan to finance 50% of the investment at a rate of interest of 12%. The business can now purchase the machine with $125,000 cash and $125,000 debt. The return on the total investment is unchanged (30%).

But now, return on the cash investment (because only $125,000 has been used, not $250,000) has increased by 18 percent to 48 percent.

The debt will cost $15,000 per annum in interest expense and will reduce the $75,000 profit to $60,000. However, dividing the profit of $60,000 by only $125,000 drives return on cash to 48%. (This example ignores income tax effect.)

The return on equity has risen even when the company has replaced equity dollars originally earning a 30 percent return with relatively expensive debt dollars costing 12 percent.

Financial leverage is a powerful amplifier. But amplifiers themselves are rather stupid. They do only that—amplify. Whatever ever you're doing, profitable or not, financial leverage will magnify the result. If the leveraged asset produces less return than the cost of the borrowed funds, the firm's losses will corkscrew downward at a head-spinning rate.

In a high growth economy or industry, leverage is generally a good thing, particularly when the borrowed money is used to finance fixed assets (plant) that will produce an unattended cash flow stream. This was the case in the cable television boom of the late 70's and early 80's.

Unfortunately and with too little foresight, entrepreneurs attempted to repeat this model in the telecommunications industry during the mid-to-late 90's. For a variety of reasons, the cash flow stream did not materialize. Therefore, the borrowers who built the plant had highly amplified expense requirements. The result was the telecom implosion of 2000.

When analyzing a particular company for potential investment, the "Debt Ratio," (total debt divided by total assets) and the "Debt to Equity Ratio," (total debt divided by equity), are important indicators of long-term solvency and risk.

Another application of financial leverage is called "Margin." Most commonly used in stock market and futures trading, Margin is the amount of money your broker will loan on a given purchase.

For example, many brokerage houses will lend 50 percent of the purchase price of a security. When positive financial leverage is in play this is good news for the investor.

However, using borrowed funds amplifies both gains and losses. You can lose more funds than you deposit in the margin account. A decline in the value of securities that are purchased on margin may require you to provide additional funds to the firm that has made the loan.

Futures, such as gold contracts, and options are even more highly leveraged instruments requiring only a small amount of money, or margin. For example, to control a great deal of gold, the initial margin on a 100 ounce gold contract (with a value of approximately $39,000) is only $2,340. Interest expense on margin loans today is approximately 0.75 percent to 3 percent. But again, leverage cuts both ways.

After you have bought or sold a futures contract, the price of the contract can go either up or down. If you start to lose money on the position you have, then you will be required to post variation or maintenance margin. If this happens, a margin call will be made requesting (more like demanding) that you deposit additional funds to keep your account within certain prescribed limits.

What's the bottom line on financial leverage? If the underlying object of leverage performs well, so will you. If the asset fails, the loss will be accelerated.

(July 2004)

Credit bureaus set up own competitor to FICO

The three major credit bureaus, TransUnion, Equifax, and Experian—are ganging up on Fair Isaac (FICO) in an attempt to break the latter's monopoly on credit scores.

They have formed Vantage Score Solutions, LLC, which has announced a new credit scorecard called "VantageScore." It purports to predict the creditworthiness of consumer borrowers.

The trio also hopes to generate more revenue for themselves by offering VantageScore and thus eliminating license fees paid to Fair Isaac.

Here's a comparative look at the two offerings.

FICO and VantageScore use two different ranges. FICO scores range from 300 to 850. VantageScore starts at 501 and runs to 990. The three credit bureaus that created VantageScore claim its range is more "intuitive." It looks a little like a school report card:

- 901-990 equals A.
- 801-900 equals B.
- 701-800 equals C.
- 601-700 equals D.
- 501-600 equals F.

Intuitive or not, the values constructed during scorecard development are arbitrary and have no bearing on the quality of the results. Introducing a new scale probably will just add to the confusion regarding how lenders use scores.

Borrowers now may try to figure out why a number that would qualify them for the best rates under one system (say, a 780 FICO) gives them a "C" grade under another.

The worth of any analytical technique is dependent upon the validity of the data. Credit-bureau data can be very different for the same person. Accounts reported at one bureau may not appear at the other two. Or a successfully disputed error at two of the bureaus may remain on file at the third.

VantageScore also aims to create comparable scores from three dissimilar databases—those of the credit bureaus. It's too early to say whether or not VantageScore is superior to FICO in this respect.

Both scoring systems rely on five classic types of data: payment history, outstanding balances, length of credit history, new credit and types of credit used.

Payment history affects about 35 percent of the total FICO score. Details regarding payments made on credit cards, retail charge cards, installment loans and mortgages are part of the calculation. Recent late payments will damage the score more than older delinquencies.

The amount owed to creditors accounts for about 30 percent of the score. Owing a lot on many accounts won't necessarily hurt the score. It's the percentage of available credit used that's critical.

The length of the credit history determines about 15 percent of the score. This part of the formula has generated concern among lenders.

New credit acquired determines about 10 percent of the score, and another 10 percent turns on the types of credit in use—the mix of installment loans, mortgages, retail accounts, credit card and finance company accounts.

Other factors make up the remaining 35 percent.

Equifax, Experian, and TransUnion are private companies that monitor consumers' accounts, balances, and payment habits. While each company has its own score, lenders prefer Fair Isaac's FICO formula.

When a lender requests a credit score—usually the FICO score—from one of the credit bureaus, the data the bureau has collected is sent through the proprietary FICO model. The bureau pays Fair Isaac for using its formula.

This is a major source of revenue for Fair Isaac. Credit scoring fees are 20 percent of the company's revenue—but 65 percent of its operating profit, according to Merrill Lynch analyst Edward Maguire.

The bureaus would prefer to eliminate the middleman. They've tried to break Fair Isaac's stronghold before, without success. However, VantageScore may be a different story.

One of lenders' complaints about the FICO model is that people whose credit histories are "thin" (they have few accounts) or "young" (their oldest account has been established for only a few months or years) still receive relatively high scores. The lenders feel that people should have a more robust credit history before they reach the top of the FICO range.

VantageScore claims it has a better way to grade people with limited credit histories. If the result is a more efficient intermediary banking system, so much the better.

On the other hand, "FICO scores are entrenched in the financial world; used by 80 percent of the 50 largest banks, 75 percent of mortgage origination decisions," said Ron Totaro, Fair Isaac's general manager for global scoring solutions. "We're a force because we've been at this for 50 years."

At the moment, consumers can't buy their own VantageScores, but Experian promises to make them available to consumers in the next few weeks, and the other bureaus say they'll do so by the end of the year.

(May 2006)

Truth in Lending Act was designed to protect borrowers

As a nation, we just celebrated our 230th birthday. That's approximately 9.2 generations of families in the United States since 1776. Our political great-great-great-great (well, you get the picture) Grandfather George Washington is famous for saying "I cannot tell a lie."

He was referring to a cherry tree and a hatchet. Our legislators have tried to carve out and cut down the amount of prevarication in our lending systems for many years.

The foundation of the modern, fiscal "I cannot tell a lie," was created just 38 years ago in the form of the Truth in Lending Act.

Congress enacted it in 1968 as part of the Consumer Protection Act. The law is designed to protect consumers in credit transactions by requiring clear disclosure of key terms in lending arrangements and every cost. The law was simplified and reformed as a part the Depository Institutions Deregulations and Monetary Control Act of 1980.

The Federal Reserve Board has implemented the law through Regulation Z, which explains how to comply with the consumer credit parts of the law. Regulation Z applies to each individual or business that offers or extends consumer credit if four conditions are met:

- The credit is offered to consumers.
- Credit is offered on a regular basis.
- The credit is subject to a finance charge (i.e. interest) or must be paid in more than four installments, according to a written agreement.

- The credit is primarily for personal, family or household purposes.

However, Regulation Z doesn't apply to business, commercial or agricultural loans.

Here are the key points (and some noteworthy warnings) of this regulation to remember when dealing with potentially dishonest lenders.

- Know the word "disclosure," and what it means.

The lender is required to disclose, meaning to tell the "whole truth" about any matter the other party should know. In most cases, failing to disclose is under penalty of perjury for "knowingly falsifying or concealing any significant fact." Disclosure is generally required before credit is extended.

Under Regulation Z, disclosure must be made of important credit terms. The four most important are:

(1) Finance charge- This is the amount charged to the consumer for the credit. It's not the interest rate. It's a dollar amount that might include items not generally thought of as finance charges, such as discount, fees, origination charges, and charges by third parties. It might even include additional principal if the structure of the loan results in negative amortization.

(2) Annual percentage rate- This is the cost-of-credit measure, which must be disclosed as a yearly percentage. It's not the stated interest rate for the loan.

This disclosure is calculated using a complex formula that measures the money coming in and going out over time, which yields the annualized "internal rate of return" (IRR) for the life of the loan.

If you're a frequent borrower, you may wish to learn more about calculating IRR by exploring this calculation in popular computer spreadsheet programs.

(3) Amount financed- This is the stated amount being borrowed in a consumer loan transaction. Be

aware that this disclosure doesn't contemplate additions to principal over time as an increase to the amount financed. This "negative amortization" becomes part of the finance charge.

(4) Total of payments- This sets forth the total number and amounts of the periodic payments by the borrower. The magnitude and timing of payments is significant to the IRR calculation above. It sets the time interval between payments for that calculation. Simply remember that the more frequent the payments, the less costly the loan.

Evidence of compliance with the Truth in Lending requirements must be retained for at least two years after the date of disclosure. Disclosures must be clear and conspicuous, and must appear on a document the consumer may keep.

You may find complete copies of these regulations and example forms at most public libraries and law school libraries. Regulation Z is in the Code of Federal Regulations at 12 C. F. R. Part 226. This regulation and many others are available on the Web at: **www.fdic.gov/regulations**.

The penalties for failure to comply with the Truth in Lending Act can be substantial. A creditor who violates the disclosure requirements may be sued for twice the amount of the finance charge. Consumers must begin any lawsuit within a year of the violation.

(July 2006)

Lenders and borrowers are circumventing banks

Commercial banks play an important role in the financial system and the economy.

Although it may not always appear this way, banks don't create money. They simply allocate funds from savers to borrowers, and reward themselves for this matchmaking effort by lending the money they receive from savers at interest rates higher than they pay to the savers (the spread), and charging fees for their connection services.

A quick glance at *The Wall Street Journal* reveals that as a saver, you'll receive about 5 percent on a one-year savings deposit. On the other hand, as a borrower, you get to pay 13 percent on an average credit card. The 8 percent difference is commercial banking's matchmaking fee.

Banks also provide specialized financial services, mostly information about both savings and borrowing opportunities. They key word is "information."

We've been living in the Information Age for awhile now. Electronic devices, high-speed telecommunication lines, and the Internet have made Alvin Toffler's "Future Shock" a reality. A simple search on the phrase "borrow money" yields 6.1 million Web site references.

Even in the face of this overwhelming information, a new form of banking has emerged, called "peer-to-peer banking." It removes most of the middleman from the process of linking savers to borrowers.

One example is a United Kingdom company called Zopa, which is an acronym for Zone of Possible Agreement. In banking, the "ZOPA" is the overlap between one person's bottom line for what they're prepared to receive and another person's top line for the most they're prepared to give.

Formed in March 2005, Zopa's service is open to any U.K. resident over 18 who passes a credit check. Rather than participate in "the spread," Zopa takes a 1 percent commission from every borrower's loan.

Since the site's debut in March 2005, more than 23,400 people have joined. "Some people hate their banks and want to borrow from real people," CEO Richard Duvall says. Zopa expects to begin operations in California before year-end.

Another example is "Prosper," which calls itself "America's first people-to-people lending marketplace." It was created to make consumer lending more financially and socially rewarding for everyone.

It operates similarly to eBay. Instead of listing and bidding on items, people list and bid on loans using Prosper's online auction platform.

People who want to lend set the minimum interest rate they're willing to earn and bid in increments of $50 to $25,000 on loan listings they select. Borrowers create loan listings for up to $25,000 and set the maximum rate they're willing to pay.

Then the auction begins as lenders bid down the interest rate. Prosper then takes the bids with the lowest rates and combines them into one simple loan. It also handles all loan-administration tasks, including loan repayment and collections on behalf of the matched borrower and lenders.

Prosper generates revenue by collecting a one-time 1 percent fee on funded loans from borrowers, and assessing a 0.5 percent annual loan servicing fee on lenders.

These companies hope that by eliminating the middleman—namely banks—individual lenders earn a higher rate of interest and borrowers get a lower rate than typically would be available from traditional financial institutions.

Users of these sites may have personal reasons for becoming involved. "I am fascinated by the concept, [and] hate big corporate banks ...," writes one Zopa user.

The fervently capitalistic appear to be better represented on Prosper, which offers lenders a wider range of risk and return. Interest rates for loans funded through Prosper range from 7.32 percent (low-risk) to 24.04 percent (high-risk)—not far from credit card rates.

Zopa, on the other hand, offers less risk and less return, claiming an average gross return of 7 percent. It reduces risk by automatically spreading lenders' money across 50 borrowers. On Prosper, lenders can form groups, but they have to manage the process themselves.

Another, perhaps even more important aspect of peer-to-peer banking is sociological. The personal preferences of individuals are far more exposed in the peer-to-peer environment, leading some to call the practice "social financing."

The value of social financing as a stable investment vehicle remains unproven. But the ability of specialty-oriented groups to offer discount loans to members of their respective communities has obvious advantages over the impersonal, institutional lending practiced by banks. Specialty-directed lending gives groups the financial muscle to advance their goals.

Prosper, for example, hosts a group called Christian Opportunities, which says it's "dedicated to helping borrowers and lenders of any denomination invest in their future." There's also the more cult-oriented Apple User Group, which bills itself as "a lending group for those wishing to purchase either a Macintosh or an Apple iPod."

(August 2006)

New Year's resolution No. 2: Pay off your debts

New Year's resolutions are a tradition dating back to the early Babylonians. The early Babylonians' most popular resolution was to return borrowed farm equipment.

According to the U.S. General Services Administration, the top three New Year's resolutions are to lose weight, pay off debt and save money.

While there may be a relationship between numbers 1 and 3 as it applies to the weekly grocery bill, let's look more closely at number 2—paying off debt.

The first step toward taking control of any financial situation is to create an accurate picture of the fiscal landscape. Start by listing income from all sources. Then record fixed expenses, such as mortgage payments or rent, car payments and insurance premiums, followed by expenses that vary, such as entertainment, recreation, and clothing.

The best course is to contact creditors directly and immediately if expenses exceed income. Explain the cause of the difficulties, and try to work out a modified payment plan that reduces monthly payments to a more manageable level. Don't wait until the accounts have been turned over to a debt collector.

Consider credit counseling. If a workable budget is hard to create and follow, creditors are unwilling to accept repayment plans, or bills continue to multiply, consider contacting a credit counseling organization. Many of them are nonprofit, and they're dedicated to solving financial problems.

The best sources for credit counseling services are universities, military bases, credit unions, housing authorities and branches of the U.S. Cooperative Extension Service—not the Internet or a telemarketer.

Be wary of credit counseling organizations that:

- Charge high up-front or monthly fees for enrolling in credit counseling or a debt-management program (DMP).
- Pressure clients to make "voluntary contributions," which is another name for fees.
- Require personal financial information, such as credit card account numbers, and balances, before sending out any information.
- Demand payments into a DMP before creditors have accepted the program.

In a DMP, clients deposit money each month with the credit counseling organization, which uses those deposits to pay unsecured debts, such as credit card bills, student loans and medical bills, according to a payment schedule the counselor develops with the debtor and creditors.

Creditors often agree to lower interest rates or waive certain fees. But the debtor should personally check with each creditor, ensuring that they offer the concessions that the credit counseling organization describes. A successful DMP requires regular, timely payments, and could take 48 months or more to complete.

There also are debt negotiation programs, which differ greatly from credit counseling and DMPs. They can be very risky and have a long-term negative impact on credit reports and, in turn, the ability to obtain credit in the future. Many states have laws regulating debt negotiation companies and the services they offer. Contact the state attorney general for more information. In Colorado, visit **www.ago.state.co.us/index.cfm**.

Debt negotiation firms often pitch their services as an alternative to bankruptcy. They regularly claim that using their services will have little or no negative impact on the ability to acquire credit in the future, or that any negative information can be removed from credit reports when their debt negotiation program is completed.

The firms encourage debtors to stop making payments to creditors, and instead, send payments to the debt negotiation company. They promise to hold funds in a "special account" and pay creditors on behalf of debtors.

If this isn't suspicious enough, remember that there are no guarantees a creditor will accept partial payment of a legitimate debt. In fact, if payments aren't received on a credit card account, late fees and interest usually are added to the debt each month.

What's more, most debt negotiation companies charge consumers substantial fees for their services, including one to establish the account with them, a monthly service fee and a percentage of the money it estimates supposedly was saved.

Watchfulness is important when considering debt negotiation. In 2004, the Federal Trade Commission charged an operation that billed itself as a debt negotiation company with pocketing the fees, thus plunging customers deeper into debt. The operation had promised to reduce consumers' debt, negotiate with creditors and stop harassment from debt collectors in exchange for various fees.

Credit-report repair is another entity. It's not the same as satisfying debts; it's usually just an attempt to make it appear as though debts are less of a problem than they are. Be very vigilant when companies promise "credit-report cleanup."

In December 2005, the Federal Trade Commission published a report titled "Credit Repair: Self Help May Be Best." Find it at:
www.ftc.gov/bcp/conline/pubs/credit/repair.htm. It's worth the read.

Hopefully this information will enable you to meet your resolution to pay off debt—and prove Oscar Wilde wrong when he said, "Good resolutions are simply checks that men draw on a bank where they have no account."

(January 2007)

PROTECTING YOUR MONEY

When I was young, I thought that money was the most important thing in life; now that I am old, I know that it is.

- Oscar Wilde

Who's protecting your money? All of these guys

It's no secret that the financial community has been under great stress the last few years. The collapse of major corporations such as Enron, WorldCom, and countless smaller firms ultimately flows directly to individual people.

Many of us may ask, "How could this happen?" "Who is supposed to watch over all of this?"

There are more than 500 government agencies (including both Federal and State levels) designed to regulate and protect financial activities. Here's a glimpse at the top eight Federal agencies charged with protecting our money.

United States Securities and Exchange Commission

450 Fifth Street, N.W.
Washington, D.C. 20549
Phone: (202) 942-8088

The primary mission of the U.S. Securities and Exchange Commission (SEC) is to protect investors and maintain the integrity of the securities markets. This is accomplished through registration requirements, disclosure of risk, and financial reporting guidelines.

Board of Governors of the Federal Reserve System

20th and Constitution Ave., N.W.
Washington, DC 20551
Phone: (202) 452-3000

The Federal Reserve's duties fall into four general areas: (1) conducting the nation's monetary policy; (2) supervising and regulating banking institutions and protecting the credit rights of consumers; (3)

maintaining the stability of the financial system; and (4) providing certain financial services to the U.S. government, the public, financial institutions, and foreign official institutions.

Comptroller of the Currency
Administrator of National Banks
U.S. Department of Treasury
Washington, DC 20219-0001
Phone: (202) 874-5000

The Office of the Comptroller of the Currency (OCC) charters, regulates, and supervises all national banks. It also supervises the federal branches and agencies of foreign banks. The OCC has six district offices plus an office in London to supervise the international activities of national banks.

Established in 1863 as a bureau of the U.S. Department of the Treasury, the OCC is headed by the Comptroller, appointed by the President, with the advice and consent of the Senate, for a five-year term. The Comptroller also serves as a director of the Federal Deposit Insurance Corporation (FDIC) and a director of the Neighborhood Reinvestment Corporation.

Federal Deposit Insurance Corp.
550 Seventeenth Street, NW
Washington, DC 20429-9990
Phone: 202-736-0000, 877-275-3342

An independent agency created by Congress in 1933, the FDIC supervises banks, insures deposits up to $100,000, and helps maintain a stable and sound banking system.

Office of Thrift Supervision
U.S. Department of Treasury
1700 G Street NW
Washington, DC 20552
Phone: (202) 906-6000

The Office of Thrift Supervision (OTS) is the primary regulator of all federally chartered and many state-chartered thrift institutions, which include savings banks and savings and loan associations. Established as a bureau of the U.S. Department of the Treasury on August 9, 1989, the OCC has four regional offices located in Jersey City, Atlanta, Dallas, and San Francisco. OTS is funded by assessments and fees levied on the institutions it regulates.

National Credit Union Administration
1775 Duke St.
Alexandria, VA 22314-3428
Phone: (703) 518-6300

The National Credit Union Administration, governed by a three-member board appointed by the President and confirmed by the U.S. Senate, is the independent Federal agency that charters and supervises Federal credit unions. With the backing of the full faith and credit of the U.S. government, the NCUA operates the National Credit Union Share Insurance Fund (NCUSIF), insuring the savings of 80 million account holders in all federal credit unions and many state-chartered credit unions.

Federal Financial Institutions Examination Council
Suite 200
2100 Pennsylvania Ave. NW
Washington, DC 20037
Phone: (202) 634-6526

The Council is a formal interagency body empowered to prescribe uniform principles, standards, and report forms for the federal examination of financial institutions by: the Board of Governors of the Federal Reserve System (FRB), the Federal Deposit Insurance Corporation (FDIC), the National Credit

Union Administration (NCUA), the Office of the Comptroller of the Currency (OCC), and the Office of Thrift Supervision (OTS) and to make recommendations to promote uniformity in the supervision of financial institutions.

National Association of Securities Dealers (NASD)
1735 K Street, NW
Washington, DC 20006-1500
(301) 590-6500

The NASD is charged with regulating the securities industry and The NASDAQ Stock Market. NASD was created in 1938 by the Maloney Act amendments to the Securities Exchange Act of 1934.

Through its many departments and offices, NASD's jurisdiction extends to over 5,300 firms with more than 94,000 branch offices, and over 664,000 securities industry professionals. NASD accomplishes this oversight through the registration, education, testing, and examination of member firms and their employees, and through the creation and enforcement of rules designed for the ultimate benefit and protection of investors.

If you have a question about protecting your money, the preceding will provide a good place to start to seek answers.

(November 2003)

Hide and Seek in Switzerland

Last month, we listed ways to keep your money secure, avoid becoming a victim of fraud and identity theft, and ways to promptly spot problem activities. Continuing with the idea of protecting your money (we hesitate to use the word hide), no instrument has received as much recognition as the secret *Numbered Swiss Bank Account.*

Here are some history and facts about this mystifying symbol of wealth and prestige.

One of the earliest pieces of legislation regulating bank secrecy dates back to the 18th Century. In 1713, the Great Council of Geneva (cantonal council) adopted banking regulations that stipulated the bankers' obligation to *"keep a register of their clientele and their transactions. They are, however, <u>prohibited from divulging this information</u> to anyone other than the client concerned, except with the expressed agreement of the City Council."*

Until 1934, bank secrecy was regulated solely by <u>civil</u> law. There were no criminal provisions; that is any threat of imprisonment for the banker at fault.

Since 1934, two articles of the Swiss *criminal code* also enforce Swiss bank secrecy:

• Article 162 regarding disclosure of trade secrets or confidential business information. It states, "Any person who has divulged a trade secret or confidential business information that was meant to be kept by virtue of legal or contractual obligation, or any person who has used this information to his or her benefit or to that of a third party, will be, on prosecution, punished by <u>imprisonment</u> or by fine."

- Article 320 deals with occupational confidentiality. It says, "Any person who has divulged a secret entrusted to him or her as a representative of authority or as a civil servant, or who has acquired knowledge by means of his or her practice or employment, will be punished by <u>imprisonment</u> or by fine."

Once the bank account is established, a number replaces your name on all documents in connection with your account. Only a few people at the bank know your identity. Your bank transfers are marked: "Bank X for the account of <u>a client</u>."

However, numbered accounts are not anonymous: the bank always knows your identity.

The numbered account offers additional protection for private matters such as inheritance or divorce, for it is up to the plaintiff to identify the bank in which the funds are deposited before the courts can pursue the case. The plaintiff's search is even more difficult with pseudonyms, such "The Prof," or "Colorado-Godfather."

What does it take to open a secret numbered account? There are two requirements.

- Minimum deposit of 100,000 Swiss Francs ("CHF"). At today's exchange rate, that's about $78,796.50. Other forms of private (though not numbered) Swiss accounts may be opened for less.
- Set-up fee of 1,299 CHF or $1,023.56

Numbered Swiss accounts also include other services such as: credit cards, mail retaining, internet banking, online trading, investments, and opening by mail. These accounts are primarily investment accounts.

Nonetheless, there are areas where even the Swiss must open the door. For example, fraud and money laundering are not welcome. Filing bankruptcy in the United States may not protect your Swiss account from creditors. In accordance with Swiss Private International Law (1987), bank secrecy can be lifted for a bankruptcy declared <u>abroad</u> when the creditor's rights have been duly established.

Because every circumstance and motivation is unique, you may want to consult some of the various legal texts that deal with Swiss bank secrecy. Swiss Federal laws that apply (more info at **www.amcham.ch**):

- Labor Code (RS 220), Article 398
- Swiss Criminal Code (RS 311.0), Articles 260; 305a; 305b
- Federal Act on International Mutual Assistance in Criminal Matters (RS 351.1)
- Federal Act on the Treaty with the United States of America on Mutual Legal Assistance in Criminal Matters (RS 351.93)
- Federal Banking Act (RS 952.0), Article 47
- Federal Act on Securities Exchanges and Securities Trading of 24 March 1995 (RS 954.1)
- Federal Act on the Prevention of Money Laundering in the Financial Sector of 10 October 1997 (entered into effect on 1 April 1998; RS 955.0)

Switzerland has ratified these international agreements (again more info at **www.amcham.ch**):

- European Convention on Mutual Assistance in Criminal Matters of 20 April 1959 (RS 0.351.1)
- Convention of 8 November 1990 on Laundering, Search, Seizure and Confiscation of the Proceeds from Crime (RS 0.311.53)
- International judicial cooperation treaties (RS 0.351 et seq.)

Of course without implying that any of these people actually have *Numbered Swiss Accounts*, you too could join the ranks of Roger Moore, David Niven, Tina Turner, and Shania Twain, all now living in Switzerland.

As we say, "*Ici vous souhaite l'énorme prospérité anonyme !*" ("Here's wishing you enormous anonymous prosperity!")

(April 2004)

What's behind identity theft—and how you can prevent it

Computer technology advances daily, maybe even every hour. Those advances make it possible for financial information to be shared more easily and cheaply than ever.

There are benefits to this increased speed. Law enforcement agencies can apprehend criminals more quickly, banks may prevent fraud, and consumers will make improved purchasing decisions.

On the other hand, as financial data becomes more accessible, precautions to protect against the misuse of information becomes especially essential. One effort to do that was *The Financial Modernization Act of 1999.*

Also known as the "Gramm-Leach-Bliley Act" or GLB Act, the legislation includes provisions to protect consumers' personal financial information held by financial institutions. The Act contains these principal parts: privacy requirements, financial privacy rule, and a safeguards rule including *"pre-texting"* provisions.

The enforcement of the GLB Act is primarily carried out by the Federal Trade Commission, (**www.ftc.gov.**) For individuals, the most valuable part is the pre-texting provisions. As listed in the Gramm-Leach-Bliley Act, it's illegal for anyone to:

• Use false, fictitious, or fraudulent statements or documents to get customer information from a financial institution or directly from a customer.

• Use forged, counterfeit, lost, or stolen documents to get customer information from a financial institution or directly from a customer.

• Ask another person to get someone else's customer information using false, fictitious, or fraudulent statements or using false, fictitious or fraudulent documents or forged, counterfeit, lost, or stolen documents.

Pre-texting repeatedly leads to <u>identity theft</u>. Identity theft is the fastest growing law-breaking activity in America; 9.9 million victims were reported last year, according to a Federal Trade Commission survey.

The most common methods of extracting money through identity theft are:

- *Credit Card Fraud* - a credit card account is opened, or an existing credit card account is "taken over";
- *Services Fraud* - the thief opens telephone, cellular, gas and electric, cable TV, or other service in the victim's name;
- *Bank Fraud* - a checking or savings account is opened in the offended name, and/or fraudulent checks are written;
- *Loans* - the crook gets a loan.

The ending result is that a person becomes liable for debts that he or she did not create. Although often publicized, it's worth repeating the basics of identity theft prevention.

- Don't give out personal information on the phone, through the mail or over the Internet unless you initiated the contact and know whom you're dealing with.
- Install caller ID on your phone. New legislation now requires that telemarketers can no longer hide their identity when making telephone calls.
- Call your financial institutions if your statements don't arrive on time. Reconcile them quickly and report any discrepancies right away.

- Keep items with personal information in a safe place. In other words, rather than let old credit cards, bank statements, and charge card receipts lie around, destroy them.
- Add <u>nonsensical</u> passwords to your credit card, bank and phone accounts.
- Be mindful about where you leave personal information in your home, especially if you are having work done in your home by others.
- Find out who has access to your personal information at work and verify that the records are kept in a secure location.
- Order a copy of your credit report from each of the three major credit reporting agencies every year.

A variant of identity theft is "affinity fraud." Con artists take advantage of being in the same club or ethnic group to prompt trust from their victims. Churches are one place where affinity fraud is increasing.

There are some early warning signs that fraud is about to occur. They include:

- The approach, whether in writing, by phone or email is unsolicited;
- There is a very short time in which to respond to claim a prize;
- An invitation to send a "processing" or "management" fee, make a purchase or sign up to a service to obtain a prize or reward;
- The need to use premium rate phone lines;
- The source of the promotion is based overseas;
- A request to send money out of the country, particularly the Netherlands, Canada, and especially countries that don't exist;
- Prizes are expressed in foreign currency;

•   An invitation to provide credit card or bank account details;

•   Rewards are wholly dependent on persuading others to join a scheme.

There's an old saying that says, "Fool me once, shame on you. Fool me twice, shame on me!" When it comes to hide and seek with our money, the preceding should help every one of us to not be fooled at all.

(March 2004)

How to protect revenues from weather's ill effects

Mark Twain said, "Everybody talks about the weather, but nobody does anything about it." We've certainly heard more talk than usual about weather in the last month because of the tragic appearances of hurricanes Katrina and Rita.

While technology hasn't conquered weather yet, our financial systems do allow participation in weather conditions in the form of "weather derivatives."

Weather derivatives are similar to other traditional financial derivatives such as commodity futures contracts, forwards, and options; except in terms of the underlying asset. While other derivatives derive their value from underlying financial assets such as gold or market indices, weather derivatives draw their value from certain measures of weather such as temperature, precipitation, wind speed, rainfall, etc.

For example, European breweries make more money when their customers can sit outside in the sunshine and leisurely drink a few pints. By buying a weather derivative, they can now hedge their losses against inclement weather. Last year, the two-week Munich Oktoberfest was hedged against rain.

Many other industries benefit from the use of weather derivatives. Utility companies can protect their volume-related revenue against cooler than average summers or unusually warm winters. Distributors of crude oil, heating oil, and propane compensate for reduced business in the winter when warm temperatures lower demand.

Agricultural companies are capable of replacing revenues that might be lost due to freeze or drought.

Insurance companies can moderate their own exposure to weather-related claims, such as was just experienced along the Gulf Coast. Financial institutions may incorporate weather derivatives as a way to broaden a client's portfolio.

The Chicago Mercantile Exchange traded the first weather contract in 1997, launching the field of weather risk management. According to Valerie Cooper, former executive director of the Weather Risk Management Association, an $8 billion weather-derivatives industry developed within a few years of its initiation.

Weather futures and options are exchange-traded derivatives that—by means of specific indexes—reflect monthly and seasonal average temperatures of 18 U.S. cities, nine European cities, and areas of Asia and the Pacific. These derivatives are legally binding agreements made between two parties, and settled in cash. Each contract is based on the final monthly or seasonal index value that is determined by Earth Satellite (EarthSat) Corporation.

In other words, just as in all commodity future contracts, one party predicts the weather will be hot and another prophesizes the weather will be cold. The contract value is $20 times the degree day index. For a complete and detailed description of the contract, visit: **www.cme.com/edu/comwea/**. Ticker symbols can be found at **www.cme.com/files/USMonthlystations.pdf**.

Due the effect of the weather on gas prices, most of us are now painfully aware that nearly 20% of the U.S. economy is directly influenced by the weather. Profitability and revenues of virtually every industry—agrriculture, energy, entertainment, construction, travel, and others—depend largely upon the wanderings of temperature.

In a 1998 testimony to Congress, former commerce secretary William Daley stated, "Weather is not just an environmental issue; it is a major economic factor. At least $1 trillion of our economy is weather-sensitive."

Weather contracts on U.S. cities are tied to an index of heating degree day (HDD) and cooling degree day (CDD) values. Both values are calculated according to how many degrees a day's average temperature varies from a baseline of 65° Fahrenheit.

For example, a day's average temperature of 40° F would give you an HDD value of 25 (65 - 40). Or, a day's average temperature of 80° F would give you a daily CDD value of 15 (80 - 65). The monthly index is the sum of the daily indices.

The value of a weather futures contract is determined by multiplying the monthly HDD or CDD value by $20. For example, if the monthly index was 208, the contract would settle at $4,160 ($20 x 208 = $4,150).

To effectively use weather derivatives, the business owner would trade as many contracts as necessary to offset the total financial impact of weather on the firm. It's primarily energy companies in energy-related businesses that use weather derivatives.

However, there is growing awareness of weather futures among agricultural firms, restaurants, and companies involved in tourism and travel.

Lest we think that betting on the weather is merely an esoteric pastime, there are over 200 Weather Risk Management Products (WRMPS) available today. Furthermore, leading companies in the industry founded the Weather Risk Management Association. WRMA is an international trade organization dedicated to promoting the industry both to those within it and to end-users.

For more information on the industry that everyone talks about, but can do nothing about, contact Weather Risk Management Association, 1156 15th Street, N.W., Suite 900, Washington, DC 20005. The phone number is, (202) 289-3800, the fax is (202) 223-9741, and the email address is wrma@kellencompany.com.

(October 2005)

Crime of embezzlement comes in many forms

Financial crimes have become so commonplace these days that *The Wall Street Journal* now has a dedicated section titled, "Executives on Trial."

Bernie Ebbers, behind the wheel of a Mercedes he had driven from Mississippi, drove into the Oakdale Correctional Complex in Louisiana on Sept. 27. Andrew Fastow, Enron Corp.'s former chief financial officer, was sentenced to six years in prison followed by two years of community service.

Both are examples of crimes arising from very complex and sophisticated legal and financial structures. They involve multiple business entities, simultaneous market trading, and interpretation of accounting rules so that true operating results were obscured and hidden.

However, the core of any financial crime is theft; taking what rightfully belongs to someone else. In the case where the thief has the right to use or hold the property of someone else, it's called embezzlement— the seed from which springs all other forms of financial transgressions.

In other words, embezzlement is the fraudulent appropriation by a person for his own use of property or money entrusted to their care but owned by someone else. For example, a clerk or cashier can embezzle money from his employer; a public officer can embezzle funds from the treasury.

Embezzlement has ranked as America's No. 1 financial crime for more than 30 years, and likely will hold that distinction for years to come. Most embezzlement cases begin with an employee covering a small, short-term financial need with the intention to give the money back. Basic internal financial controls can prevent or substantially reduce the opportunity for this to occur.

There are dozens of embezzlement schemes.

"Lapping" is one classic embezzlement scheme. It involves stealing a customer's payment on an account and concealing the theft by applying subsequent payments from other customers to the first customer's account.

Another classic scheme is through fabricated vendors or consultants. Any employee with authority to approve the payment of invoices can perpetrate this method.

In larger organizations, a midlevel employee may be able to approve invoices. The thief creates imaginary vendors and deposits checks written to pay the false invoices into his or her personal bank account.

In a recent case involving a large trade association, the CFO is alleged to have embezzled $2.5 million from the organization during a 13-year period through recurring payments to phony consultants.

Theft of cash receipts is the simplest form of embezzlement, usually perpetrated by insiders, simply by pinching incoming cash or highly negotiable instruments. This is particularly true in organizations that deal with a large number of relatively small transactions, such as utility payment processing centers and collection agencies.

Payroll fraud and embezzlement is where the embezzler adds the names of relatives or fictitious people to the company payroll, thus enjoying several salary checks each week instead of one.

Some other examples, and things to look out for, include:

- Pocketing cash payments from customers and not posting the charge or payment.
- Opening a checking account under a false name, then writing a "customer refund check" to that name.
- Handing the busy executive a stack of checks to sign, including an extra one.
- Falsely recording past-due accounts as written off or settled, then collecting from the customer.
- Purposely paying a bill twice, then intercepting and pilfering the resulting refund.
- Manipulating account balances through online computers, making "adjustments" to accounts, particularly dormant accounts.
- Hiding merchandise, cash, computer data, and account information in the trash for later retrieval by an accomplice.
- Always making a copy of the bank statement first, and then using white-out to change the balance to cover what was taken.

Jarmila Pencikova with Osler, Hoskin & Harcourt LLP of Toronto, and Doug Miller with Kahn Kleinman, LPA in Cleveland, presented the following profile of an embezzler:

(1) Completely trusted and never checked,
(2) Several years service with firm,
(3) Rarely takes vacation/holidays,
(4) Secretive and rarely delegates to others,
(5) Personal/family health or financial problems,
(6) Lifestyle inconsistent with income,
(7) Rumors of an affair or drug/alcohol abuse,
(8) An unusually close relationship with vendor.

Generally, these embezzlers are motivated by greed, fear, denial, and revenge. Many thieves steal from their employers as a way of getting revenge for actions the employer has taken that the employee believes to be unjust, discriminatory, or corrupt.

A KPMG survey in 2002 reported that the average incident goes on for 18 months before detection.

More than half the time, the crime is exposed only through a tip or by accident. Furthermore, less than 11 percent of embezzlers are caught as a result of external audits.

As business owners, individual investors, and customers of potential embezzlers, it behooves us to pay attention to the basics. Offshore bank accounts, special-purpose corporations, and off-balance sheet accounting make for interesting reading.

But they're all just a form of stealing called embezzlement.

(October 2006)

THE INEVITABLE TAXING OF YOUR MONEY

Intaxication: Euphoria at getting a refund from the IRS, which lasts until you realize that it was your money to start with.

> - From a *Washington Post* word contest

Paying too much in taxes? Some steps you can take

It's a new year, often the occasion for two things: resolutions and income taxes.

Benjamin Franklin left us many proverbs to ponder, particularly around the turn of a new year. One "resolutionary" admonition is, "Each year one vicious habit discarded, in time might make the worst of us good."

If paying too much income tax is a "vicious habit," here's some promising news for 2006.

A new year brings us all closer to retirement. A fresh saving tool, the Roth 401(k), is now available. Starting in 2006, you are able to designate part or all of your 401(k) contribution to a Roth 401(k), if your employer's 401(k) plan allows it. All income from Roth plans will be tax-free when withdrawn at retirement.

You can contribute up to $15,000 (or $20,000 if you're 50 and over) into a Roth 401(k), as opposed to only $4,000 (or $5,000) in a regular Roth.

For those interested in discarding the vicious vehicle vice of SUVs, the deduction for buying a hybrid-powered automobile increases to $3,400 in 2006, generating a tax credit that varies by make and model. For example, a Toyota Prius generates a $3,150 bottom-line credit; the Ford Escape's credit is $2,650. These credits are limited to the first 60,000 hybrids the manufacturer sells.

In 2006, the gift tax exemption rises to $12,000, up from $11,000 last year.

Parents often give those gifts to their children as a way of avoiding estate taxes. In 2006, $2 million will be estate tax-free, up from $1.5 million in 2005. The estate tax is scheduled to be discontinued in 2010.

If improving your primary residence this year, some items will qualify for a 10 percent tax credit. For example, new skylights, outside doors, windows or pigmented roofing, high-efficiency furnaces, water heaters and central air conditioners. However, the credit is limited. The maximum credit is $500 with no more than $200 attributable to windows.

Additionally, a 30 percent credit is available for the cost of solar energy systems to heat the air or water in your home. Unfortunately, pools and hot tubs don't count. This credit is limited to $2,000 apiece for home furnaces and water heaters, but is available for vacation homes as well.

Though the sales tax deduction and the teacher's deduction were to be discontinued at the end of 2005, they may be extended. Sales tax and teacher's supplies receipts will be necessary to claim the deductions.

For those who may not have atoned for past vices, the Internal Revenue Service has a broad-based, limited-time opportunity for taxpayers to come forward and settle an array of transactions the IRS considers abusive. Taxpayers have until Jan. 23 to submit their settlement documents to the IRS.

The initiative, described in Announcement 2005-80, identifies 21 transactions eligible for the program. Consisting of both listed and nonlisted transactions, they include a wide collection of schemes involving funds used for employee benefits, charitable remainder trusts, offsetting foreign currency option contracts, debt straddles, lease strips, and certain abusive conservation easements.

All eligible transactions carry the same settlement terms except the applicable penalty level. Further details on the 21 covered transactions are available in publication FS-2005-17 (**www.irs.gov/newsroom**).

Another 2005 initiative extended into 2006 is relief for taxpayers affected by the major hurricanes. Deadlines for affected taxpayers to file returns, pay taxes, and perform other time-sensitive acts have been postponed until Feb. 28. Additional details are available at the above Web site.

Beginning Jan. 1, the standard mileage rates for the use of a car (including vans, pickups or panel trucks) increased to 44.5 cents per mile (up from 40.5 cents) for business miles driven. The rate is 18 cents per mile for medical or moving purposes, and 14 cents per mile driven in service of charitable organizations, other than activities related to hurricane relief.

Some good news: The IRS announced there would be no change in the interest rates for the calendar quarter that began Jan. 1. The interest rates remain as follows: 7 percent for overpayments (6 percent in the case of a corporation); 7 percent for underpayments; 9 percent for large corporate underpayments; and 4.5 percent for the portion of a corporate overpayment exceeding $10,000.

Again, in the words of Benjamin Franklin, "Certainty? In this world nothing is certain but death and taxes."

But also, "The Constitution only guarantees the American people the right to pursue happiness. You have to catch it yourself."

Happy catching in the New Year.

(January 2006)

A dozen ways to save taxes—all of them illegal

It's tax preparation time. As the clock ticks inexorably toward April 17 (two extra days this year because the 15th is a Saturday), thoughts of big refunds are inescapable. Predictably, there are also other people who would like to skim some of your refund by providing tax "advice." Some of that advice may be phony.

Here are a dozen popular ploys that could cost you money—or land you in jail.

(1) Create Imaginary children. The earned-income credit offers lower-income workers a way to save on taxes—particularly if you're supporting two or more children. Unscrupulous tax preparers sometimes "borrow" one client's "extra" offspring and transfer them to another filer's return to illegally manufacture this tax break.

(2) Pretend you're a church. In this swindle, con artists convince individuals to apply for incorporation (called a "Corporation Sole") under false religious pretexts so they are entitled to exemption from federal income taxes as a nonprofit, religious organization. Con artists have been charging up to $1,000 or more per person to sell the details of this tax-avoidance scheme.

(3) Someone steals you. Identity theft is the No. 1 consumer complaint, and the crime can easily escalate during tax season. The IRS is aware of several scams involving taxes or the IRS. In one, tax preparers allegedly used client information, such as Social Security numbers and financial data, to commit identity theft.

(4) The lemming scam. "I don't pay taxes. Why should you?" Con artists boast about how they don't file or pay taxes. They're happy to share their "secret"—for a fee. "Un-tax yourself for $49.95." If you buy this con and accompanying how-to material, you'll ultimately find yourself out a lot more money. You'll hand over the price of the fake tax-saving secret and face civil and criminal tax penalties.

(5) All I do at home is business. The home-based business must be legitimate. Don't necessarily believe—or pay—promoters of work-at-home plans that purport to make all your personal expenses tax-deductible. Businesses must have a clear business purpose and profit motive to claim business expenses.

(6) Form 2439 rip-off. People offering tax credits or refunds related to reparations for slavery have deceived thousands of African-Americans for years. There is no law that allows for any slavery-related tax breaks. Mention of Form 2439 (Notice to Shareholder of Undistributed Long-Term Capital Gains) is the warning sign.

(7) Distrusting trusts. This tax season, abusive trust schemes are the No. 1 scam. Promoters increasingly urge taxpayers to transfer assets into trusts. Promises include bogus benefits such as reduction of income subject to tax, deductions for personal expenses paid by the trust and a decrease in gift or estate taxes.

(8) Snake-oil return preparers. Unethical return preparers hoodwink customers by diverting a portion of the taxpayer's refund for their own benefit. Tax return preparation shouldn't be performed on commission.

(9) Zero withholding. These swindles rely on an interpretation of tax law that wages are not a "source" of income and that the definition of "sources of

income" doesn't apply to individuals. If anyone brings up Section 861 of the tax code, walk away.

(10) Wade in the water. Hiding income in offshore banks and brokerage accounts, or using offshore credit cards, wire transfers, and foreign trusts isn't a good idea. This scam was No. 1 during the 2003 tax season. It's still near the top, but concentrated IRS efforts in this area (along with an amnesty program last year) yielded more than $170 million in taxes, interest, and penalties associated with illegal offshore accounts.

(11) "Claim of Right" doctrine. Under what con artists are calling the "claim of right," perpetrators of this tax dodge assert that a taxpayer can deduct all of his or her wages as "a necessary expense for the production of income" or "compensation for personal services actually rendered." The IRS says this scam is "based on a complete misinterpretation of the Internal Revenue Code and has no basis in law." Try it, and you'll hear from an auditor.

(12) Fantasy zeros, imaginary time. Some filers enter zero income, but report their withholding and then write "nunc pro tunc"—Latin for "now for then"—on their return. It may as well be Greek, because the IRS still will come after you.

The Federal Trade Commission works for the consumer to prevent fraudulent, deceptive, and unfair business practices in the marketplace, and to provide information to help consumers spot, stop, and avoid them.

To file a complaint or to get free information on consumer issues, visit ftc.gov or call toll-free, 1-877-FTC-HELP (1-877-382-4357), TTY 1-866-653-4261.

The FTC enters Internet, tax preparation, telemarketing, identity theft, and other fraud-related complaints into Consumer Sentinel, a secure, online database available to hundreds of civil and criminal law enforcement agencies in the United States and abroad.

(February 2006)

How to avoid IRS trouble, as the tax deadline nears

It's March Madness, the time of NCAA basketball tournaments. College basketball fans across the country hope their favorite team will emerge victorious from the Final Four.

It's also the final full month of tax-preparation season.

Millions of taxpayers also hope their final tax returns aren't one of the estimated 1.5 million returns chosen for audit. Here are things to scrutinize so that your 1040 filing is more like a relaxed free throw than an exasperated flail from half-court.

First, a little bit of back-to-basics regarding income reporting.

- Report all your income on the proper forms and on the correct lines. For example, W-2 income belongs on Form 1040, line 7; income from residential or office rent goes on Schedule E; and 1099-MISC non-employee compensation should appear on a Schedule C, etc.

The IRS utilizes automated matching techniques. If you receive a W-2 or 1099, (especially a 1099-B), the sender also has filed a copy with the IRS. It's important to show all the amounts on your return to avoid unmatched records in the IRS's computer systems.

- 1099-INTs are particularly tricky. Report the income on Schedule B exactly as it appears on your 1099-INT, rather than combining it under one heading. You may be asked to explain why you haven't reported it all when, in fact, you have.

- Include tips and cash payments on your return, especially if your profession is known to involve substantial currency payments. Underreporting your income is the most dangerous audit invitation.

▪ Declare hobby income on Form 1040, line 21 rather than attempting to take hobby expenses as a business loss on Schedule C. Hobbies vs. business draw the attention of auditors.

▪ Annual income over $100,000 makes you special in the eyes of the IRS. During the fiscal year 2005, audits of taxpayers taking home more than $100,000 annually reached 221,000.

To remain inconspicuous in the deduction arena, heed the following.

(1) Keep charitable donations proportionate to your annual income. IRS Service Center computers can, and do, compute means and standard deviations. For non-cash contributions, such as donating college textbooks to the local library, avoid inflating the value. Automating matching tools abound to generate comparisons of donated items.

(2) Self-employed persons or small-business owners draw an inordinate amount of attention. The self-employed are tempted to blur the distinction between personal and business expenses, such as a mileage deductions or designating the basement of your home an office.

Generally avoid the home office deduction if you can. An arms-length lease agreement with your own small corporation avoids this potential exposure.

(3) The IRS closely looks at unusually high deductions compared to your own income. If you earned $100,000 from your day job, but "invested" in the real estate market and claimed an $80,000 loss, you might become an audit candidate. Systems look for offsetting deductions against reported income.

(4) Deductions and expenses on your return also are weighed against other taxpayers in the same income bracket. Many tax-preparation software programs will do these calculations for you based on known averages.

(5) Double check for inadvertent duplicate deductions across Schedule-A, Schedule-C and Schedule-E.

(6) If you know the deduction exceeds the average, file an explanation with your return. For example, if your tenants damaged rental property, list repair costs under "Other Expenses: Tenant Damage" rather than under the generic "Repairs." In extreme cases, attach a copy of a document that will substantiate your deduction.

(7) While some audits are random, most are the result of statistical comparisons. Though one large deduction can trigger an audit, the taxpayer has the right to take all legitimate deductions, and questions can be answered by providing adequate documentation.

(8) Finally, make your return easy to handle. File electronically instead of hand-writing your return. Avoid attaching unnecessary forms to your tax return unless you absolutely have an extraordinary situation.

According to the Internal Revenue Service:

- Audits of individuals with incomes over $100,000 surpassed 221,000, the highest figure in 10 years, and well over double the 92,000 completed in fiscal year 2001.
- Audits of small businesses organized as corporations numbered 17,867 in 2005, up from 7,294 a year earlier.
- Audits of larger corporations—those with assets of more than $10 million—increased 14 percent from a year ago to 10,878.

And one last shot in overtime: The No. 1 factor that draws attention to your filing remains—believe it or not—forgetting to sign the return.

(March 2006)

Wait: There still are tax deductions for procrastinators

There always seem to be many tax advice columns right before the end of the calendar year. While some of us spent New Year's Eve celebrating and toasting the annual rotation of the human odometer, others were busily writing last minute (and hopefully deductible), checks in fervent attempts to minimize unpleasant events on April 15, 2005.

For example, buying a large SUV for business before December 31st generated a deduction of up to $100,000. First-year deductions for such a purchase in 2005 are now capped at $25,000.

Additionally, you will no longer be able to deduct non-cash donations over $500 (including a car, boat or plane) unless you've received documentation from the charity indicating whether the property will be sold or used by the organization. You will only be able to deduct the amount the charity receives from the sale.

Hopefully you got your donation into the hands of your favorite charity by December 31.

But in the time-honored spirit of procrastination, there's still something you can do to minimize 2004 tax liabilities. This is particularly pertinent to *Individual Retirement Accounts.*

Although 2004 contributions to 401(k)s and 403(b)s are still required by Dec. 31st, contributions (generally limited to $3,000) to a deductible IRA may still be made until the due date of your tax return. Just be certain to notify the trustee that it is a 2004 contribution.

The extended date of the tax return (which can be as late as Oct. 15, 2005) is the cut-off for making 2004 contributions to a SEP (Simplified Employee Pension) or SIMPLE (small employer sponsored) IRA.

Taxpayers turning 50 before the end of the taxable year that meet the Modified Adjusted Gross Income (MAGI) requirements for the Traditional or Roth IRA are allowed to make an additional $500 contribution to the regular contribution as long as you have earned income to support the excess amount.

Consider using a cash advance from a credit card to make the contribution. The IRS considers the expense deductible in the year that the charge is incurred, not when you pay the credit card bill.

Remember, you cannot contribute into your IRA more than you earned income. If such contributions exceed the limits for that tax year, they are classified as "excess contributions" and the owner may be subject to an excise tax on them.

Excess contributions can be corrected by withdrawing the excess amount any time up to the due date of the return. If the excess amount is withdrawn during the specified period, it is as if the contribution was never made, and no excise tax is due.

As you can see, tax legislation is encouraging a focus on retirement. If you have exhausted the above measures for the 2004 tax year, now is the time to at least formulate some changes for 2005.

Become involved with your employer's retirement plan and open an IRA. In 2005 there are increased retirement contribution limits. The maximum IRA contribution limit will increase from $3,000 to $4,000 and the maximum 401(k) and 403(b) employee contribution limit will increase to from $13,000 to $14,000.

Also, beginning in 2005 the IRA deduction *income phase-out* is increased by $5,000. If you are covered by a retirement plan at work, you can <u>also</u> take an IRA deduction if your modified adjusted gross income is less than $80,000 (married filing joint) or $60,000 (single or head of household); as opposed to $75,000 and $55,000 in 2004.

One a final note: double check your withholding level. The Internal Revenue Service announced that in the fourth quarter 2004, individuals will pay 5 percent interest for underpayments on taxes, an increase of 1 percentage point from the previous quarterly level.

If all this seems baffling, just remember:

"A tax loophole is something that benefits the other guy. If it benefits you, it is tax reform." — Russell B. Long, U.S. Senator.

"I am proud to be paying taxes in the United States. The only thing is, I could be just as proud for half the money." — Arthur Godfrey, entertainer.

"People who complain about taxes can be divided into two classes: men and women." — Unknown.

"Next to being shot at and missed, nothing is really quite as satisfying as an income tax refund." — F. J. Raymond, humorist.

Here's wishing many refunds of the day. Happy New Year.

As always, please check with your CPA, or tax advisor to confirm that any suggestion made here is applicable to your situation.

(January 2005)

MOVING MONEY AROUND

Money is like manure; it's not worth a thing unless it's spread around encouraging young things to grow.
                    - Thornton Wilder, "The Matchmaker"

If there's so much money available, where is it?

According to Applied Reasoning, Inc. (an economic indicator research firm), there was $1.19 trillion in the U.S. money supply on September 8, 2002. If you're like many businesses these days, you might ask, "OK, so where is it?" In order to answer that question, we must examine two basic components of the economic system. They are money and velocity.

Most of the time we talk about money in terms of simple amounts. Such as, "I have $10,000 in savings," or "I need $35,000 to buy that car." However, underneath those statements is the implied definition of "fiat" money: something that represents control over goods and services. The $10,000 in savings is meaningless unless it is connected to some item or service that we desire. It's really not the $35,000 we want; it's the car. Money has no value if it doesn't move from one person to another. The rate at which the money moves is called velocity.

What makes an economy thrive is not just how much money there is, but rather the rate at which it travels between people and organizations. We've all heard the term "money is tight." That statement is more than just a clever catch-phrase. It means—of that $1,192 billion dollars—not much of it is moving around.

The money supply turns over on average about three times a year. When economists fail to predict the future, it's not because they don't know how much money has been created by the Federal Reserve Board and released through the banks. It's because they don't know what people are doing with it. When people feel threatened, they put their money in the bank and the velocity goes down. When they feel good about life, they buy everyone a beer and the velocity goes up.

The velocity of money is affected by two sophisticated sounding terms: "propensity to save, and propensity to spend." Two other words that might be used are "keep" and "give." The velocity of money is directly affected by more than one person's (or company's) willingness to *give*; which implies an exchange for something of value, rather than simply *keep*. As this is repeated from one entity to another it's called the "multiplier effect." That is, person A gets $10, keeps a dollar and gives $9 away, hopefully in exchange for something useful. Person B gets $9, keeps 90¢, and gives the rest away, and so forth. Continuing with the original keep/give ratio of 10%, 50 exchanges will multiply the initial $10 into almost $90 in economic activity. That's what makes the economy either thrive or throttle.

There is little doubt that today's financial climate is not encouraging. There doesn't seem to be any money. That is not quite a true statement. The basic amount of money in the system has not dramatically changed. It is simply stuck. Velocity has dropped to what some might call a snail's pace.

In order to stimulate a faster velocity of money, or in other words motivate people to "give" rather than "keep," a variety of fiscal and monetary tools are usually employed. The Federal Reserve Board uses interest rates as a tool to stimulate or slow the velocity of money. It is discouraging to see that recently this utensil of lowering interest rates has not had an immediate effect on the velocity of money and hence economic stimulation. Fiscal and monetary policy may not be enough for today's conditions. The bottom line lies with those who are keeping the money.

A recent phenomenon in business is that many of the same services are being performed, and at the same rate as two years ago. But, the providers of the services are not being paid. For example, a consultant provides services to a client. That same consultant engages an attorney to provide services to him. The client doesn't pay the consultant and the consultant doesn't pay the attorney. The same services were rendered between the parties and the work was done but the only thing created were accounts receivable and accounts payable. No cash (money) changed hands. Removing the "monetizing" layer reveals that the real measure of economic activity may reside in accounts receivable/payable growth, which is directly reflective of just how much work is actually being performed. Maybe the Department of Commerce should be measuring that.

If fiscal and monetary policies are having no effect and work is still being performed, then "Where has all the money gone?" It's stuck. It's stuck with people and institutions for emotional reasons that have little to do with traditional financial evaluation. Interest rates could be virtually zero, but unless someone makes an intentional decision to spend based upon both intellectual and emotional confidence, the money will stay stuck.

(October 2002)

The strange relationship between war and money

At first glance, it might seem that the marriage of war and money is nonsensical. However, war does seem to improve economic conditions. In fact, commerce and military conflict have been linked together for many centuries. In 1828 Webster <u>defined</u> war as: "A contest between nations or states, carried on by force, either for defense, or for revenging insults and redressing wrongs, for the <u>extension of commerce</u> or acquisition of territory. . ."

Without commenting at all on the political, ethical, emotional, or moral issues surrounding war, there are economic relationships that often lead to an improved fiscal climate. Of course using statistics alone may not reveal factors such as: perceived uncertainty, expectations and the propensity to spend, or willingness to invest.

Nevertheless, it is worth exploring both the obvious and not so obvious relationships that make the process of war economically stimulating.

Classic economic fiscal policy theory tells us government spending stimulates the economy because it puts more funds into circulation.

Add to that the multiplier effect—that is, one new dollar (less what each person saves) passing from person to person has an influence of $10 or possibly more. It's the government that pays for war.

Some of the expenditures are obvious. It's easy to see the benefit for manufacturers of wartime equipment and supplies. The campaign requires vehicles, food, transportation, communications, ammunition, clothing, gasoline, etc.

However, some of the fiscally stimulating expenditures are less obvious.

Members of the military assigned to or deployed to a combat zone receive additional "combat pay" (officially called "imminent danger pay") which also carries a tax advantage. Congress and/or the President can designate combat zones as "Tax Exempt" areas.

Earnings received while in these combats zone are excluded from taxable income. Bonuses and "special pays" are also excluded from taxable income if earned in the same month while in a combat zone.

In addition, members of the military in a combat zone are authorized to deposit up to $10,000 (per year) of their pay and allowances into a special savings account that pays a guaranteed 10 percent interest per year.

This program was established during the Vietnam era, and then phased out at the end of the Vietnam War. It was revived in 1991 during the Gulf War and still exists today.

This means that the government spends more for its military labor in times of war while simultaneously employing the additional fiscal policy tool of tax reduction and preferential return. These policies increase available money to be placed into the economic structure.

However, one set of parameters does not represent the entire model. Fiscal, monetary, and psychological issues mix together in a highly intricate and multifaceted way. Though government spending supposedly stimulates the economy, governments have no real income other than through taxation.

Robert Shapiro of MSNBC reminds us that since democratic governments are reluctant to ask their citizens to pay much higher taxes while they're also placing their people in mortal peril, most large wars also involve changes in monetary arrangements to finance the conflict.

America's first national currency and modern bond operation grew out of the Union's financing schemes for the Civil War. World War I funding demands transformed the infant Federal Reserve from a lender of last resort in bank panics into a modern central bank. The deficit financing of the Vietnam War (and monetary policies to accommodate it) helped launch the inflation of the 1970s.

To try to quantify the magnitude of the war relative to the entire economy, consider the following relationships.

President Bush has requested $74.7 billion from congress to finance the first installment of the war, which is $20 billion, more than the $54 billion AOL Time Warner lost in the 1st Quarter of 2002. Some have estimated the cost of the war will be more than $300 billion.

According to the U.S. Department of Commerce, Gross Domestic Product (the output of goods and services produced by labor and property located in the United States) was $10,586 billion at the end of 2002. That means the estimated expense of the war is approximately 3 percent of GDP.

Money and war—strange but inextricably bound bedfellows. The etymology of the word "war" comes from the Old High German *werran* to "confuse." At war's end, maybe clarity will return.

(April 2003)

'Check 21' act: dramatic changes to use of checks

The Check Clearing for the 21st Century Act went into effect Oct. 28. The Act, known as "Check 21," encourages the banking industry's use of image technology to create electronic versions of checks, called Image Replacement Documents (IRD).

The law also changes the manner in which checks are processed and returned to the creator.

This new law removes the requirement that banks handle paper. Instead, banking institutions may process electronic images of your original checks.

The time between writing a check and its being paid is known as "float." Under Check 21, checks that you write will be processed in a matter of hours (maybe even seconds), not days. In the past, typical float times were between two and four days. That time lag is now virtually gone.

Businesses and individuals commonly utilize float to their advantage. Banks themselves even offered predictive services so customers could keep their funds in interest-bearing accounts until the last possible moment.

Float taken to the extreme is called "kiting." Kiting is the process of moving imaginary money within the check-clearing cycle. For example, you have $10 in bank A but you write a check on the account for $500 and deposit it in bank B. Before that deposit can be processed, you go back and tell the teller at bank B that you want to withdraw $400. The teller gives you $400 in cash, and you disappear before the check bounces.

Another service that will change is the "stop payment." With such fast processing times, it will become harder to prevent a check you've written from being paid. With just a few hours to enter a stop-payment notice, the ability to control purchase rescission and high-pressure conflict situations is greatly diminished.

Under the new act, any bank in the processing sequence can convert your paper check into an electronic image, discarding the original. Canceled checks that are converted into an IRD won't be returned with your statement and are unrecoverable from your bank.

However, IRDs have the same legal standing of an original check. Presenting an IRD will serve as presenting the original. Banks routinely save copies of canceled checks (and IRDs) for seven years.

On the other hand, there isn't yet a limit on what banks will be allowed to charge for providing electronic checks. You may also have more difficult time proving fraud. Pen pressure or ink color variations are common fraud-detection techniques.

The banking industry has known for quite awhile that electronic check processing could save perhaps as much as $2 billion a year. Under previous law, financial institutions normally needed to return paper checks to the issuing bank in order to be paid, moving them by air, truck and courier. Check 21 eliminates this transportation cost. At $200 billion in checks processed every business day, this is an enormous savings for banking institutions.

Another important piece of the Code of Federal Regulations, namely Title 12, Section, 205, Regulation E, now becomes even more critical. The Electronic Fund Transfer Act, "... establishes the basic rights, liabilities, and responsibilities of consumers who use electronic fund transfer services and of financial institutions that offer these services. The primary objective of the act and this part is the protection of individual consumers engaging in electronic fund transfers."

Here are some recommendations for dealing with the changes brought about by Check 21:

- Use a debit card for in-person transactions. Debit cards are covered under Regulation E, which gives you the powerful "right of re-credit." If a mistake is made in the transaction, the bank must resolve the problem or put the disputed amount back in your account within 10 business days.

- However, if the card will be out of your sight, such as at a restaurant, use a credit card instead. Though banks will restore any money stolen using your debit card within a few days, you may temporarily have an empty checking account.

- Use automatic debit for recurring bills. Although still resisted, you actually have more rights under Regulation E to deal with any errors related to automatic debit than when writing a check. Now that float will be a thing of the past, the advantage to paper checks has disappeared.

- Use online bill payment. Again, Regulation E protects electronic payments. If you use online bill payment, take steps to keep yourself safe, such as not using public computers or wireless hotspots for financial transactions and keeping your anti-virus software up to date.

For more information and suggestions, visit NACHA, the Electronic Payments Association at ecc.nacha.org.

(November 2004)

Your shopping is what really stimulates U.S. economy

December is a "magical month." It's filled with holiday events, office parties, family gatherings, concerts, annual correspondence with friends, decorating, and festive reminiscence of years gone by.

But for those of us focused on money, the most important event in the magical month of December is shopping.

Buying presents, flying cross-country to visit relatives, having special dinners and parties— consumers spend more money in the three months before New Year's than at any other time of the year. In fact, retailers often make about half of their annual profit during this time, according to the National Retail Merchants' Association.

Real median household income remained unchanged between 2002 and 2003 at $43,318, according to a report by the U.S. Census Bureau. Of that amount, $702 will be spent on celebration-related items. That's 2 percent of total income.

In a survey conducted by the National Retail Federation, those polled said they expect to spend the bulk of their $702 holiday budget—or about $407—on family members. Consumers will splurge $71 for friends, $41 on those such as babysitters, teachers and clergy, and $22 on co-workers.

Holiday shoppers will also not forget themselves. The poll found consumers will spend an average of $89 on "self-gifting."

The expected $702 spent on the holidays this year is 4.5 percent more than 2003. According to Manpower, Inc., 38 percent of wholesale/retail chains surveyed plan to increase holiday staff this season, up from 32 percent last year and the largest percentage since 2000.

There are approximately 108 million households in the United States. Therefore, by just doing the math ($702 times 108 million) we might naively say that the holidays contribute $75 billion in economic activity.

However, it's not just the amount of money in the system that makes a robust economy; it how fast it's moving.

For example, of the $20 you pay for a box of greeting cards, $18 may go to the company that produced the cards for sale. Of that $18 the printing company received, $14 may be paid to employees-- $12 will be spent on holiday cards, and the cycle speedily repeats.

This creates a statistic known as the *multiplier effect*. On average, the money supply turns over about three times a year. That means that for each $1 spent on holiday items, the economic effect is actually $3. Our $75 billion just expanded to $225 billion. Applying the multiplier effect to the money supply ($1.4 trillion as of 3rd quarter), we find that the holidays move 6 percent of that currency around per year.

Much of the buying now will be on credit. During November and December, credit card balances tend to balloon by about 4 percent of disposable income. That's not surprising, given that banks mail over 3 billion credit cards solicitations each year to American consumers.

It's also not too surprising, then, that many people are so carried away during this festal time that they can't dig themselves out for months or even years.

Credit cards generally require 2 percent to 3 percent of your current balance each month as a minimum payment. For a $1,000 balance, that's $25. But if you pay $25 a month at the average interest rate of 18 percent, you'll be burdened by this year's holiday purchases well into the next year. And you'll end up paying hundreds of dollars in interest on that $1,000.

That's appalling news for the consumer, but excellent news for the financial markets. A portion of the interest you pay is placed back into monetary circulation by the credit granting company in the form of loans to other customers; stimulating more economic action.

"It has been the American consumer—the American household—that has been the main driver behind economic growth," said Rick Kaglic of the Federal Reserve Bank of Chicago. "Consumer spending, despite the volatility, remains healthy."

These factors influence consumer spending:

• Low interest rates, which make big-ticket items such as cars more affordable.

• Increasing value of household assets.

• Competitive retail pricing. "Retailers (are) doing just about anything they can to get people to come into their stores and walk out with merchandise," Kaglic said.

• Consumer confidence, although there has been a slight decline because of rising oil prices and slow job creation.

Whether households continue to spend at the same level will depend on how much money workers are earning. But Kaglic sees an encouraging sign: Wage and salary growth increased 0.4 of a percentage point in August. That number seems small, said Kaglic, but it's better than economists have seen in the past.

So as we head into this year's magical month of December, help the country prosper. Do what Kaglic says: Keep shopping!

(December 2004)

Give a public company to person who has it all

It's the time of year when many of us contemplate gifts for our friends and family. Choosing a gift for some will be harder than for others.

For the business person in your life who seems to have everything, how about giving them a public company?

Many entrepreneurs have the goal of one day becoming "public." That is, their stock publicly trading on one of the exchanges. The traditional initial public offering (IPO) to become publicly traded involves a lengthy accounting, legal, and underwriting process. Costs can be $500,000 to $1 million.

However, a technique called "reverse merger" may allow a private company to become public in a fraction of the time—just in time for the holidays.

In a reverse merger, the private company's shareholders purchase control of a public shell, possibly for as little as $35,000. A public shell is a publicly listed company with no assets or liabilities. All that exists of the original company is its corporate structure. By merging into such an entity, a private company becomes public.

The transaction can be accomplished within weeks, resulting in the private company becoming a public one. If the shell is a reporting, SEC-registered company, the private entity avoids much of the expensive and time-consuming review process with state and federal regulators, because the public company already has completed the process.

Upon completion of the reverse merger, the name of the shell company usually is changed to the name of the private one. If the shell company has a trading symbol, it's changed to reflect the name change.

An information statement, called an 8-K, must be filed within 15 days of the closing. The 8-K describes the newly combined company, stock issued, information about officers and directors, and audited financial statements. The 8-K must disclose the same type of information required when registering a class of securities under the Securities Exchange Act of 1934.

If the shell company is already listed on the NASDAQ Bulletin Board exchange, the registered or "free trade" shares can continue to trade. To trade new shares, the newly combined public company must first register the shares with the SEC. This process takes three to four months and normally requires filing an SEC Registration Statement SB-2 or SB-1.

If the shell company doesn't have a symbol, an application for a symbol is typically made to the NASDAQ Bulletin Board. The application for a symbol requires filing a Form C211 by a member of the National Association of Securities Dealers.

Although reverse mergers are receiving more scrutiny from the SEC than in the past, there remain advantages, including:

- Due to the liquidity available through the public exchanges, publicly traded companies enjoy substantially higher valuations than private companies.
- Raising capital is frequently easier because of the added liquidity for the investors, and it often takes less time and expense to complete an offering.
- The time required to secure public listing is considerably less than that for an IPO.
- The costs are significantly less than the costs required for an initial public offering.

- No underwriter is needed. This is a significant factor to consider given the difficulty smaller companies face attracting an investment banking firm to commit to an offering.
- Acquisitions with public stock are often easier and less expensive.
- Lack of an earnings history doesn't normally keep a privately held company from completing a reverse merger.
- Stock options or stock incentives can be useful in attracting management and retaining valuable employees. In extreme cases, special stock known as S-8 stock may be issued to employees in lieu of regular salary.
- Public company stock provides a long-term exit strategy for the founders and is easier to use in estate planning for the principals.

However, disadvantages of going public (including through a reverse merger) are:

- Complete (and expensive) financial disclosure is required for publicly held companies under the SEC regulations.
- There are substantially higher costs of regulatory compliance for the audit, legal and investor relations work.
- Owners of the private company often give up some equity percentage in the merger (usually between 15 percent and 20 percent).
- Management must devote additional time to public company activities.
- Increased visibility brings a higher level of liability exposure.
- Founding management may become distracted by the opportunities owning publicly traded stock offers. The distractions can become so severe,

management might even forget to keep running the business.

There are thousands of Web sites explaining and offering assistance for reverse mergers. Many are investment consultants who also are selling public shells. Some of the more well-known are:

- **www.gopublicintheusa.com**
- **www.reversemerger.com**
- **www.keatinginvestments.com**

Local author James Arkebauer, founder of Venture Associates (**www.venturea.com**) in Denver, has written an excellent book: "Going Public: Everything You Need to Know to Take Your Company Public, Including Internet Direct Public Offerings" (Dearborn Financial Publishing, $29.95), available at bookstores.

(December 2005)

Cost of currency can be an unpleasant surprise

"Money" is defined as "something generally accepted as a medium of exchange, a measure of value, or a means of payment, as in officially coined or stamped metal currency." "Fiat" means "authorization." Fiat Money is legal tender, especially paper currency, authorized by a government. We use "Fiat Money" in this country in the form of United States Dollars—bread, dough, cash, lucre, bucks, lolly, loot, shekels, smackers, rocks; you get the picture.

In economic terms, money represents command over good and services. But, here's the chafe. In our ever shrinking world, where technology provides almost instant access to any country on the planet, the "unit of exchange" for command over goods or services is often unique to that particular nation. This gives rise to an entire industry called currency exchange.

Many of us are familiar with the British Pound, Japanese Yen, even Indian Rupees, but in addition, there are over 40 other commonly exchanged currencies.

They are: American Dollar, Argentine Peso, Australian Dollar, Bahraini Dinar, Botswana Pula, Brazilian Real, British Pound, Canadian Dollar, Chilean Peso, Chinese Yuan, Colombian Peso, Czech Koruna, Danish Krone, Euro, Hong Kong Dollar, Hungarian Forint, Iceland Krona, Indian Rupee, Iraqi Dinar, Israeli New Shekel, Japanese Yen, Malaysian Ringgit, Mexican Peso, Nepalese Rupee, New Zealand Dollar, Norwegian Kroner, Omani Rial, Pakistan Rupee, Polish Zloty, Qatari Rial, Saudi Riyal, Singapore Dollar, Slovenian Tolar, South African Rand, South Korean

Won, Sri Lanka Rupee, Swedish Krona, Swiss Franc, Taiwan Dollar, Thai Baht, United Arab Emir. Dirham, and Venezuelan Bolivar.

This gives rise to three levels of complexity facing persons involved in international activities.

- The delineation of "command over goods and services" changes dramatically within regions. The cost of gasoline for example, is simply higher in some parts of the world than others, no matter what currency is used.

- Currency exchange is based upon varying rates and usually requires an intermediary, similar to a stock broker. There is a cost associated with doing the basic conversion. The fee is similar to an "origination fee" in lending.

- Market forces and perceptions cause fluctuations in exchange relationships amplifying any real economic change.

For the privilege of exchanging dollars into Swiss francs, a fee of up to 4 percent may be applied. That is, if while preparing for your trip to Geneva to buy some chocolate, you convert 1,000 USD into Swiss Francs (1,346 CHF as of today), you will pay $40. While this may be a small sum for the occasional traveler, for on-going business is can represent a significant impact on profits.

Using a credit card is a convenient way to accomplish currency exchange while traveling abroad; however, it is not free. Furthermore, since the conversion is performed automatically, the cost is not immediately recognized.

American Express and a handful of major banks, including Citibank, the USA's largest credit-card issuer, have added surcharges of up to 5% on purchases made in foreign currencies.

Further obscuring the real cost of conversion, many banks use their own "exchange rates." The exchange rates have the fee built in and are often different from the "spot price" of the given currency. Spot prices, or "foreign exchange mid-range rate," are based upon banks exchanging currencies in amounts of $1 million or more.

Unless you take the time to check the exchange rate quoted in *The Wall Street Journal* (always on the back-page of Section C), or through the Internet by using a site such as XE.com, the disparity would never be revealed.

Currencies are in essence a commodity in themselves. Various factors, not unlike those affecting the perceived price of pork bellies or orange juice cause fluctuations that become a risk factor for international dealings.

In February of this year MetaFilter, Inc. reported that, "The Federal Reserve's greatest nightmare is that OPEC will switch its international transactions from a dollar standard to a Euro standard. Iraq made this switch in Nov. 2000, and has made out like a bandit considering the dollar's steady depreciation against the Euro. The dollar declined 17% against the Euro in 2002."

Companies can now use a broad range of financial arrangements to reduce or eliminate their currency exchange risk exposure. The most widely used instruments are the forward market and options. Commonly listed futures options in currency include: Japanese Yen, Canadian Dollar, British Pound, Swiss Franc, and Euro Dollar.

Leaving aside the accounting difficulties that an international corporation must deal with, any individual is well advised to consider the cost of currency exchange before making any exchange transaction. It can be an unwelcome surprise and there are no refunds—only more expensive exchanges.

(September 2003)

TIMES OF TOO LITTLE MONEY

My problem lies in reconciling my gross habits with my net income.

- Errol Flynn

A few do's and don'ts for dealing with a cash crunch

According to the *Cambridge Dictionary of American English, "crunch" is defined as:* a difficult situation that forces you to make a decision or act. **Crunch time** is a point at which something difficult must be done. For example, *He plays fine without pressure, but can he produce at crunch time?* When there isn't enough cash to pay current obligations, it's polite to say, "We're having a *cash crunch*." That is, we're in a difficult situation requiring hard decisions about how to disperse the cash that is available.

In order to make survivable decisions during a cash crunch, various factors must be considered: legal, operating requirements, staff retention, and public relations to name just a few. Some of these factors are lofty and rather strategic in nature; others just plain survivorship. In fact, if you are contemplating the mixture of spending between inventory and sales activities, some may say, "you don't know what a genuine cash crunch is." The crunch is really on when you contemplate whether you can run the business just using everyone's personal cell phones.

Although every set of circumstances is different, here are some dos and don'ts for surviving *Cash Crunch Time*.

Stay out of jail. It is extremely tempting, particularly if you believe things will improve relatively soon, to delay making employer wage withholding tax payments. Don't do it. It is better to pay some employees properly than to pay all workers hoping that the tax payments can be made up later. The term "net check" should not be in your vocabulary. Federal Code penalties in this area are severe; enforcement mechanisms are powerful and carry personal liability to officers. Likewise, delaying payments into 401(k) plans or cafeteria benefit plans (no matter how optimistic you might be feeling) can snowball into much larger problems.

Revisit insurance policies. Many insurance policies (particularly product liability) are based upon estimated annual sales. If you're in a crunch, those estimates may in fact be too high. Talk with the carrier and have the premiums recalculated based upon a lower projection. Not only will the premiums be reduced, but, you may also be able to switch from large lump sum payments to a monthly payment plan. Deductible limits may be adjusted as well—the higher the deductible, the lower the premium. Raising deductibles does shift more risk to you, but it will help conserve cash in the near-term.

Don't be distracted by unsecured noise. A cash crunch requires hard decisions; decisions based upon business issues, not emotional outpourings. The old adage "The squeaky wheel gets the grease," applies here. Some creditors are apt to make loud verbal threats and employ other intimidating tactics. Don't be distracted by empty verbal assaults. Rather, evaluate each requirement against the genuine damage that could be caused by the creditor. Although certainly not optimal, creditors that have a security interest in your operation need to be addressed before those that are unsecured.

Do consider S-8 stock. If your company is publicly traded and fully reporting, you may be able to register additional shares of stock on SEC form S-8. This is a special registration of stock for the specific purpose of compensating employees or consultants for their efforts. However, be very careful of the rules regarding who may accept S-8 stock. Without doubt, S-8 is a powerful tool: it empowers fully reporting companies to register shares quickly and easily—without automatic SEC examiner review. S-8 registration allows issuers to compensate employees and some outside consultants with registered shares in lieu of cash. S-8 shares cannot be issued in connection with capital formation or promotion of the company's shares and must be issued to natural persons for bona fide services.

Don't ignore the problem. It's a rare person or business that hasn't experienced a cash crunch. They are not fun and can be embarrassing and a severe test of patience. Nevertheless, you must communicate with each person. Left to their own devices and in the absence of any information from you, creditors will spin out the worst-case scenario and escalate their positions. It's a simple rule: return every phone call, answer every letter. During a cash crunch, "No news is **not** good news." A better euphemism is "love me or hate me, but don't ignore me."

Use deposits. It's highly likely that when you entered into the office lease, initiated gas and electric service, or telephone service that you put a certain amount of money on deposit. This may be the time to request use of those deposits. Certainly not a permanent solution, but the Lessor or provider of service may be willing to use the deposit for a period of time and then allow you to build it up again.

Request extensions. Many lenders, especially secured ones understand the cyclical nature of cash flow. During a cash crunch, you may find certain lenders amenable to "extending" their loans. That is, no payments for a period of months (often 2 or 3), in exchange for putting those payments at the end of the loan. Frequently this can be accomplished by a simple phone call. Of course, it will take longer to pay off the loan, but it helps you through the crunch.

The preceding suggestions are not a permanent solution for an ailing business. Underneath these cash crunch techniques, there must be a viable business model and tactically sound management practices that will eventually enable profitability. In the meantime, hang on and keep your cell phones charged.

(November 2002)

Who's 'slipping out the back' in bankruptcy

In the 1975 song *"50 Ways To Leave Your Lover,"* Paul Simon sang, "Just slip out the back, Jack, Make a new plan, Stan; You don't need to be coy, Roy; Just get yourself free; Hop on the bus, Gus; You don't need to discuss much; Just drop off the key, Lee; And get yourself free."

The financial equivalent of those lyrics is the U.S. Bankruptcy Code, specifically Title 11 of the U.S. Code of Federal Regulations (CFR). For example, "Slip out the back, Jack" could mean Chapter 7 liquidation, "Make a new plan, Stan" might be Chapter 11 reorganization.

Here's a closer look at the corporate bankruptcy process.

Federal bankruptcy laws govern how companies shut down or recover from crippling debt. The company that's in trouble—the "Debtor,"—might use Chapter 11 of the Bankruptcy Code to "reorganize" its business and try to become profitable again.

Management continues business operations but all major business decisions must be approved by a bankruptcy court.

Under Chapter 7, the company terminates all operations. A *Trustee* is appointed to liquidate the company's assets and the money is used to pay off the debt, which may include debts to creditors and shareholders.

In a bankruptcy, assets are divided in this order.

- *Secured Creditors* - often a bank, is paid first.
- *Unsecured Creditors* - such as banks, suppliers, and other lenders, have the next claim.

- *Shareholders* - owners of the company, have the last claim on assets. Existing shareholders may not receive anything if the Creditors' claims are not fully repaid.

Many companies will file under Chapter 11 rather than Chapter 7 because they can still operate and have some control over the bankruptcy process.

Bankruptcy papers consist of a two-page "Petition," a 15 to 21 question *Statement of Financial Affairs*, and schedules showing: Real Property, Personal Property, Property Claimed as Exempt, Creditors Holding Secured Claims, Creditors Holding Unsecured Priority Claims (Taxes, etc.), Creditors Holding Unsecured Non Priority Claims, Executory Contracts and Unexpired Leases, and Co-debtors.

In addition, a Chapter 11 Debtor needs to file a list of the 20 largest unsecured creditors, including the creditor's name, address and telephone number.

The filing of the Petition creates an automatic prohibition, "stay," against virtually any action to pursue any claim against the Debtor or any assets without first obtaining court approval.

Occasionally companies prepare a reorganization plan that is negotiated and voted on by creditors and stockholders before they actually file for bankruptcy. This abbreviates and simplifies the process.

If the pre-approved plan entails an offer to sell securities, the securities may have to be registered with the SEC. Shareholders will get a prospectus and a ballot.

It's important to vote. Under the Bankruptcy Code, two-thirds of the shareholders who vote must accept the plan. Dissenters will have to go along with the majority.

Without a pre-approved plan, the *Trustee* often appoints one or more committees to represent the interests of creditors and shareholders to collaborate with the company to develop a plan of reorganization to get out of debt. The plan must be accepted by the creditors and stockholders. The bankruptcy court must confirm the plan.

Committees of creditors and stockholders negotiate a plan with the company to relieve the company from repaying part of its debt so that the company can try to recover. However, even if creditors or shareholders vote to discard the plan, the court can disregard the vote and still confirm the plan. The plan must treat creditors and shareholders fairly.

One committee that must be formed is called the "official committee of unsecured creditors." They represent all unsecured creditors.

An additional official committee may sometimes be appointed to represent shareholders. The Trustee may appoint an additional committee to represent a distinct class of creditors, such as secured creditors, employees, or subordinated bondholders.

After the committees work with the company to develop a plan, the bankruptcy court must evaluate the plan to guarantee that it contains no fraud and complies with Bankruptcy Code. This is the "plan confirmation," process; usually taking a few months to complete.

Although a company may emerge from bankruptcy as a viable entity, generally, it is the creditors and the bondholders, not the existing shareholders that become the new owners of the shares.

In most cases, the company's reorganization plan will cancel the existing equity shares because secured and unsecured creditors are paid from the company's assets before common shareholders.

In situations where shareholders do participate in the plan, their shares are usually subject to substantial dilution.

The Legal Information Institute or the Cornell Law School has an excellent website containing the complete U.S. Code, at http://lii.law.cornell.edu.

Of course, the relative appeal of bankruptcy is largely dependent upon which side of the "bus" you're on; creditor or debtor. For every "Jack that slips out the back," there's a Jill left holding the bag.

(October 2004)

The new way to survive a personal bankruptcy

President George W. Bush recently signed the Bankruptcy Abuse Prevention & Consumer Protection Act of 2005, ("BAPCOP"). The new law takes effect October 17, 2005.

"By restoring integrity to the bankruptcy process, this law will make our financial system stronger and better," Bush said in a news conference.

That sounds reassuring. However, everything in today's financial and economic systems are intertwined, and no one action provides a complete path toward improvement.

The following explores some of the history and implications relating to bankruptcy and the new regulations.

The first official laws concerning bankruptcy were passed by England in 1542, under Henry VIII. A bankrupt individual was considered a criminal, subject to criminal punishment. Potential penalties ranged from incarceration to death.

U. S. bankruptcy laws for the protection of debtors were first enacted in 1800. However, the foundation of modern bankruptcy law and practices in the United States began with the Bankruptcy Act of 1898.

The economic turmoil of the late 1920's and early 30's spawned more bankruptcy legislation, notably, the Bankruptcy Act of 1933 and the Bankruptcy Act of 1934. This legislation culminated with the Chandler Act of 1938. From 1938 to the present day, bankruptcy laws and procedural rules continued to be refined.

The Bankruptcy Reform Act of 1978 created Chapter 11 reorganization and a more powerful form of personal bankruptcy, Chapter 13. In 1986, Chapter 12 was created for family farms.

Enter now BAPCOP of 2005. The American Bankruptcy Institute estimated that up to 210,000 people will be affected by BAPCOP—unless they file for bankruptcy before October 17.

The major modifications provided by this Act are as follows.

Income test. Income is subject to a two-part "means test" to determine if the debtor can afford to pay 25 percent of their "non-priority unsecured debt" such as credit card bills. Then income will be compared to the debtor's median income. If income is above the state's median and the debtor can afford to pay 25 percent of the unsecured debt, the debtor may not be allowed to file under Chapter 7 liquidation. However, Chapter 13 reorganization may still be available.

Charitable tithing. Up to 15% of one's income can be given to charity; a possible loophole allowing people who may be just over the threshold of having to file Chapter 13 to drop down low enough to file Chapter 7.

Child support and alimony. These debts become number one on the priority list as opposed to seventh under the old law.

Homestead exemption. Currently, some states allow debtors to protect some or all of their home's equity from creditors. The new Act, however, places restrictions that are more stringent on the homestead exemption.

Creditors' rights. Currently, creditors who won't receive any money owed in a bankruptcy case may contest the ruling if it's a Chapter 7 case, but not if it's

Chapter 13. Creditors may now challenge Chapter 13 filings as well.

Liability for lawyers. Under the new law, bankruptcy attorneys may be subject to various fees and fines if the filings are found to be inaccurate. The increased liability will make lawyers less willing to accept bankruptcy cases and if they do, costs will no doubt be higher.

Credit counseling. In a provision similar to required parenting classes in divorce cases, the new bankruptcy law requires credit counseling in the six months prior to applying for bankruptcy, and money management classes. The debtor pays for these classes.

Multiple filings. The time between effective Chapter 7 bankruptcy filings in creases from six years to eight years.

Automatic disclosure. Additional disclosures are required from debtors. Although debtors need to provide trustees with essentially any documents concerning their financial history under Bankruptcy Rule 2004, this Act makes the disclosures automatic, required, and mandatory. Otherwise, the case will be dismissed.

Audits. Random audits performed by certified or licensed public accountants must be done on .04 percent of filings of personal Chapter 7 and 13 cases, and on cases that vary from statistical norms. Furthermore, the discharge of debts may be denied if the debtor fails to cooperate with the auditor.

The results of these changes in the law will of course not be known for several years and opinions about the new law are expectedly varied.

Bob Waldschmidt, former president of the National Association of Bankruptcy Trustees, called the up-front credit counseling requirement a waste of time, but likes the bill's requirement that, before leaving bankruptcy, filers take a course in managing household finances.

"This is not going to be as drastic as people make it out to be," he said. Still, he added, "the system is going to get more expensive and burdened with more work."

(May 2005)

Downsizing – what about those Left Behind?
An upside for the "downsized-in"

Nobody wants to be downsized (unless of course it's as a result of some involvement with Jenny Craig). Of course, in all our political correctness the actual acceptable phrase is "Rightsizing." Now what the heck does that mean? Were we the wrong size a minute ago? Will the company become more politically conservative? Will there be a reaction of West Coast companies "Left-sizing?"

But enough of this linguistic blather; downsizing means that some people got laid off, given the boot, kicked out, given the opportunity for career enhancement, separated from the firm, are now absent, the company is now a lean, mean, commerce machine. Some people are gone, and others remain.

Regardless of how the situation developed, you may in fact find yourself among those "left behind," faced with handling a challenging and stressful situation. Studies have demonstrated that starting a new job is more stressful than being laid off. After a downsizing, you are in many respects starting a new job. Often there is an assumption flying around that after a downsizing, things are expected to remain the same. The same amount of work product produced with fewer people. This is false. Change was called for. It's no longer a case of work harder; it's a call to work *smarter*. Focus on what is truly needed; items that are critical to survival and progress; not simply critical to documenting the demise. Ask the question, "Is this a productive activity or a documenting activity?"

For example, back in the early days of computer systems it was soon discovered that computers could produce more reports than previously even dreamed of in the half-slumbering minds of the most obsessive-compulsive manager. Therefore, more and more reports were automated, became fruitful and multiplied. After a period of time however, a systems analyst would ask, "Why are we producing all these reports? It's interfering with our *adventure* game playing on the computer." No amount of surveys, questionnaires or polite inquiries could produce sufficient excuses to stop producing all those reports.

One way to discover what's certainly critical is to stop producing everything and let business issues themselves determine where energy should be spent. Management mandated change—as a remaining member of the squad, manage that change.

Don't take it personally. As Michael Corleone said, "business is business and you're taking this personally, Sonny!" Although all of us spend a great deal of time <u>doing</u> our jobs, we <u>are</u> not our jobs. That applies both to those that are now gone and those that remain. It will do your mental health little good to speculate on the philosophical reasons of why, wherefore, and how come, and if only… Remember, the game now is to work smarter, not harder. Harder will only make you tired, smarter may in fact help bring about the new environment.

Stand up for your compensation. It's highly probable that after a downsizing you will have more and wider responsibilities. You may have even absorbed the work of an entire department. In other situations, this would often mean additional cash compensation. Expecting that in the recently downsized company is an exercise in an ulcer. It's like the bank charging you more of what you don't already have when you bounce check. Cash is not available. However, other forms of compensation are (or should be), and if not, should be vigorously sought.

If your responsibilities have widened, create and obtain a new title for yourself. The best way to do this is to find a title that listed in one of the many salary surveys published by state agencies or personnel firms. There is a reason for this. Once business conditions improve, you will have an automatic basis for receiving additional cash compensation based upon those salary guidelines associated with your new title. In other words, compensate yourself now by setting your stage for when the company emerges from its difficulties.

Remaining with a troubled company is not fun. However, it does not have to be a death sentence. Downsizing means change. Change means that something will be different. That difference will be most positive for you if you focus on what's important, recognize that management are people too, realize that the reason why is irrelevant, and don't expect fairness or logic. Now is an ideal time to rearrange your own stage for when the curtain rises on the second act.

(August 2002)

Are creditors at your door? Tips for keeping them at bay

During trying economic times, companies and individuals can often find themselves with more debt than can be comfortably handled. In turnaround situations, the income stream of a company can fall below the required payments on its debt. For individuals, this usually means they can't make their minimum payments on credit cards. In financial circles, monthly payments are called debt service. When debt isn't serviced, creditors are naturally less than thrilled.

If the debt goes unserviced for too long, you will no doubt have the opportunity to make new friends who work in the collection industry. Here are some tips, insights, and suggestions for successfully handling creditors and collectors.

Don't take it personally. It will help you to remember that a collection call, no matter how unpleasant, is a business transaction. It's not an assault on your personal character. However, it is a frequent practice for collectors to attempt to intimidate and scare you. Remember that many collectors are paid based upon what they collect. Therefore, keep all conversations to the point, professional, and focused on the debt; not irrelevant passive-aggressive personal invective.

Return every phone call. Federal law prohibits collection calls before 8 a.m. and after 9 p.m. Nevertheless, many hard-hitting collectors would like to catch the debtor late in the day or early in the morning when they may be more susceptible to emotional pressure. Let the answering machine work for you at those times. But, when you're ready, emotionally detached, and prepared to deal with it, return each and every call, even if it's just to say, "I have nothing today." Not responding to phone calls will escalate your account through the collection process, quickly becoming unmanageable.

Remember your rights. In 1996, the Fair Debt Collection Practices Act (FDCPA) was enacted. It specifies that debt collectors cannot harass you. Specifically collectors cannot: call your office, call your home before 8 a.m. or after 9 p.m., address you in an abusive manner, or call family or friends in an attempt to collect the debt. If you have an attorney, the collector may not contact anyone except your attorney.

If you do not have an attorney, a collector may contact other people but only to find out where you live and work, but usually not more than once. In most cases, the collector is not permitted to tell anyone other than you and your attorney that you owe money. These protections should be held in your mind, not used as some arsenal to win a battle. After all, you do owe the money.

However, if there continues to be a problem with collectors contacting other people concerning your debt, you can file a complaint with The Federal Trade Commission, Sixth and Pennsylvania Ave., NW, Washington, D.C. 20850, phone: 202-326-2222.

You have already paid for some conciliation. Without going into an extensive dissertation on interest rate theory, bear in mind that unless you are paying about 1.5 percent on your loan, the creditor expects some delinquency. The risk structure of interest rates includes allowances for the creditor's expected delinquency, liquidity, maturity and default risk. If your loan has an interest rate greater than 9 percent and you have a history of prompt payment, you have already paid for your delinquency. This thought might be helpful in working out a plan for the creditor to receive their real rate of return.

Be ready to make a deal. Most creditors will be glad to negotiate a lower amount on the total bill you owe because it is better for them to get some money than none. Even if the loan is secured, it is often more desirable on the part of the creditor to renegotiate the loan than to seize and liquidate the collateral. This is particularly true with hospitals, credit card issuers, and automobile dealers.

Tell the truth. Collection situations are never cheerful. As tempting as it may be to make a promise based upon a hopeful event, it will not help the situation at all. It is far better to say, "I don't know" than to say, "Oh, the money will be coming next Tuesday." Or even worse, "The check's in the mail." (With the advent of electronic processing, many collectors will tell you that the mail is so slow, your payment cannot possibly reach them in time, so just do an electronic transfer.)

Based on truthful statements, creditors have suspended debt service for up to six months; allowing the company to work out of the difficulty. At the end of the day, the only people that will fail in business are those who are incapable of adopting an approach of rigorous honesty.

As our economic climate improves, so will our ability to service debt. By invoking the items above you will be able to manage out of tough times and be ready to exploit the opportunities of the next surge in fiscal activity.

(June 2002)

EVALUATING THE MONEY

Beauty is in the eye of the beholder.

- Paraphrase of Plato

Seven ways to determine what your business is worth

There are a number of reasons for valuing a business—sale or purchase of the entity, estate and tax purposes, and for raising capital. If a company is public, these valuation methods have nothing to do with the stock price.

The worth of a business is based upon two major factors: the assets owned by the concern (tangible or intangible) and the income stream being generated by the firm's operations. In other words, static property owned or continuing money flow from operations.

Within those two broad categories, the seven methods below will facilitate constructing a reasonable value.

1. Particularly in the high-technology industry, the value of a company may be based primarily on one **specific static asset value**; often the intangible asset is intellectual property.

This approach is usually based upon the buyer's desire for a particular intangible asset; frequently a new proprietary technology protected by patent or trade-secret. The price offered will reflect the buyer's assessment (often not revealed to the seller), of the expected profit from the asset. The best example is Bill Gate's purchase of the first PC operating system, which launched Microsoft.

2. In some instances, a business is worth no more than the fair value of its tangible assets, or "**liquidated value.**" Valuing a business in this way is simply a matter of obtaining the best possible price for the equipment, inventory, and other assets of the business. An interested party in a similar industry may want the

assets left in place. "In place" value is generally higher than on a piece by piece basis at auction.

3. The **leapfrog startup** approach is used when the purchaser wants to avoid the difficulties of starting from scratch. The buyer calculates the start up requirements in terms of dollars and time, including projected costs to organize personnel, obtain leases, obtain fixed assets, and the cost to develop intangibles such as licenses, copyrights, and contracts.

A reasonable premium may be offered because of the effort and time being saved by the buyer. The more difficult, expensive, and time-consuming getting underway is likely to be, the higher the value based upon this method.

4. One of the most common flow-method approaches to valuation is the use of a **market value multiplier.** When analyzing gross sales, gross sales plus inventory, or after-tax profits of comparable businesses in the industry, a multiplier is applied to create a value. Obviously, the construction of the multiplier is critical. This method is similar to price-earnings ratios used is stock price evaluation.

One industry rule of thumb says an Internet Service Provider company is worth $75 to $125 per subscriber plus equipment at fair market value. Another says that small weekly newspapers are worth 100% of one year's gross revenue.

5. For mature companies, **capitalization of earnings** is appropriate. The Capitalization Rate is the *expected return on investment* to the investor or purchaser.

This technique of valuation is suitable for established service companies and other non-asset intensive businesses that have few if any, fixed assets.

The basic formula determining capitalized earnings is: projected earnings divided by capitalization rate equals value. The capitalization rate is a probable risk level.

A reasonable capitalization rate considers factors such as the length of time the company has been in business, longevity of current ownership, reasons for selling, operating and legal risk factors, profitability, location, barriers to entry and exit, level of competition, industry potential, technology, and others.

6. The **excess earnings method** is similar to the capitalization method described above except that returns from fixed assets are separated from other earnings—hence "excess" earnings.

The two capitalization methods work for businesses that receive their income primarily from tangible assets such as a utility or stable manufacturing concern. In the case of businesses that earn only a small part of their revenues from tangible assets, the excess earning method is probably a better method to use.

7. Using the **cash flow method** is most appropriate when one firm desires to acquire another firm in the same industry and borrowed funds will be used to consummate the transaction. Therefore, the evaluation will center on how much of a loan the cash flow will support. Typically, profits are adjusted for depreciation, amortization, and an estimated annual amount for equipment replacement.

If cash flow is, for example, $1 million and prevailing interest rates are 10 percent, and the loan is amortized over 5 years, the value would be $3,922,110. On a fully amortized basis over 5 years, total interest is about $1,000,000.

Determining the value of a business is more of an art than a science and it is not precise. Ultimately, the value is the result of face-to-face negotiation between the seller and buyer.

(February 2005)

Assets—in the eye of the beholder

The poet said, "Beauty is in the eye of the beholder." What possible application would that soft and lovely expression have in the hard indifferent world of finance? It means a great deal when it comes to the relative worth, or "beauty" of your firm's assets. Another related poetic phrase, though not nearly as engaging, is "One man's trash is another man's treasure."

We all have assets that are surely treasures to us. They are something beautiful that we hold. The *American Heritage Dictionary* provides the following definitions for <u>assets</u>: 1. A useful or valuable quality, person, or thing, an advantage or resource; 2. A valuable item that is owned; 3. In accounting, the entries on a balance sheet showing all properties, both tangible and intangible. Assets can include cash, stock, inventories, property rights, and goodwill.

What are those assets worth? In the very end, after all the GAAPs, SAPs, FASBs, and other variations of accounting rules and statistical analysis, an asset is worth simply this: What did someone pay you for it. This might be a great excuse to introduce the "greater fool" theory, which states that no matter what you have, there's someone who is a greater fool than you are willing to buy it!

If you own something and really want to know its worth—sell it. That's the bottom line. .

As we traverse the complex world of finance there are circumstances where we'd like to be able to show someone else what assets we have so that our "worth" might be calculated. The measurement might be made in order to induce additional investment into our firm, obtain a loan against these assets, or simply to feel good about how we've spent the better part of our lives. Whatever the reason, our "assets" are our treasures—to others maybe they're just rubbish.

APB 17 specifically addresses "intangible" assets; that is, things that may produce wonderful results but that cannot be felt, touched, lifted, or shipped by truck, such as the value of intellectual property (one of the most important intangible assets), technology licenses, and other agreements.

In more elevated terms, *Intellectual Property* is defined as "original creative works that have economic value." Principal types of intellectual property are patents, copyrights, and trademarks. Other types of intellectual property also include trade secrets (i.e. Coca-Cola soft drink formula) and the right of publicity (i.e., a famous athlete may profit by using his/her name to endorse a product). Intellectual property is similar to an intangible asset because both are intangible in nature. Since intellectual property is similar to an intangible asset, it is often used interchangeably.

Our accounting standards specifically state, ". . . a company should record as assets the costs of intangible assets acquired from others, including goodwill acquired in a business combination. A company should record as expenses the costs to develop intangible assets that are not specifically identifiable. The Board also concludes that the cost of each type of intangible asset should be amortized by systematic charges to income over the period estimated to be benefited. The period of amortization should not however, exceed forty years."

What does this very erudite statement really mean? This: If you acquire an asset, that is (from the definition above) a valuable person, quality or thing, you may record that value at its hard cold cost. Period. For example, if you paid $10 for an invention that would ultimately allow *star-trek* transport systems actually to work, the asset that would appear on your balance sheet with a value of $10.

However, if someone <u>gave</u> you that asset (no strings attached and therefore no cost), you would be faced with valuing that asset based upon predicted cash flow profits from that asset.

As an example, UAL (United Airlines) reported $3,738,000,000 in revenue for the period ended September 30, 2002. Consequently, if your company were <u>given</u> (at no cost to you), an asset that replaced air travel and the firm expected to capture only half the market, your balance sheet could be the recipient of a $1,869,000,000 asset!

Based upon United States accounting policy, that $10 piece of trash on the one hand is, in the twinkling of an eye, poof!—a multi-billion dollar treasure. Needless to say and before the entire accounting profession is up-in-its-arms, there are many more subtleties and complexities that may come into play. Nevertheless, the beauty of an asset remains in the eye of the beholder. For that reason, be careful what you stare at, you may actually get it!

(March 2003)

CONFUSING MONEY

If all the economists were laid end to end, they'd never reach a conclusion.

- George Bernard Shaw

Trying to comprehend the dichotomy of dividends

For years there has been a dichotomy surrounding dividends. Fundamentally, it's because while dividends represent an attractive characteristic for investors seeking income (rather than growth) from their portfolios, dividend payments are not a tax-deductible expense for the company issuing them. At the same time, dividend income is taxable to the person receiving them at the time of delivery. This creates the infamous "double dividend tax."

Another way to look at it is Company A earns $100, pays out $25 of tax-deductible expense, pays tax on $75 at 34 percent of $25.50 leaving a return of $49.50.

Company B earns $100, pays tax on $100 at 34 percent of $34, and then pays a dividend of $25 making its return $41; $8.50 lower than Company A with the same earnings. In addition, the receiver of the dividend from Company B pays tax on $25 as income.

To maintain "tax efficiency" corporate tax avoidance (not to be confused with evasion), has increased. Firms are engaging in strategies that are more aggressive to shield income from taxation through tax shelters and other means.

A recent analysis published by the National Bureau of Economic Research found that the gap between what corporations report as profits to their shareholders and the profits reported to the IRS for tax purposes has grown sharply over the past decade.

The study finds that $154 billion cannot be explained by traditional accounting differences, indicating higher levels of sheltering activity.

Most firms try to follow a consistent dividend policy. This attracts investors who seek a stable, dependable income. However, dividend payments are not guaranteed. More than one company has found itself in trouble by continuing to pay dividends when earnings were too low.

There is currently a great deal of attention focused on dividend tax relief. Many believe it will provide a substantial economic revival; both in this country and around the world.

Thirty nations around the world belong to the Organization for Economic Cooperation and Development ("OECD"). Nearly all major nations allow full or partial relief of dividend double taxation, and thus have lower maximum dividend tax rates than the United States. Indeed, the latest data show that the United States has the second highest dividend tax rate in the Organization. The top U.S. rate of 70.1 percent surpasses every country except Japan. Mexico, imposes an upper rate on dividends of just 35 percent— half the top U.S. rate.

Overall, 27 of 30 OECD countries have adopted one or more ways of reducing or eliminating dividend double taxation. Only Ireland, Switzerland, and the United States do not provide relieve from this double taxation.

On the other hand, Ireland and Switzerland have corporate tax rates of merely 12.5 percent and 24.5 percent, respectively, much lower than the U.S. federal corporate rate of 35 percent.

One common method of dividend tax relief is to set the tax rate on dividends lower than the ordinary rate on wages. Austria, Belgium, Italy, Korea, the Netherlands, Poland, Portugal, and Sweden use this approach.

Another methodology is to provide an individual dividend exclusion. Germany and Luxembourg provide a 50 percent exclusion. Greece provides a 100 percent individual exclusion, which is currently being proposed by President Bush.

Numerous countries provide individuals a dividend tax credit to offset the corporate tax paid on the earnings. Canada, France, and the U.K. offer partial credits. Nations providing credits that fully offset double taxation include Australia, Finland, Italy, Mexico, New Zealand, and Norway.

Many say that the most straightforward way to address the inequity would simply be to provide corporations with a full deduction for dividends paid. Currently, the Czech Republic and Iceland allow a partial dividend deduction to corporations

Historically in the United States, between 1954 and 1986, the income tax code included various exclusions for dividend income. In some years, the code also provided a further credit for a percentage of dividend income in excess of the excluded amount. Starting in 1954, the first $50 of dividend income ($100 for married couples) was excluded along with a credit incentive. Beginning in 1965, only a fixed-dollar exclusion was retained. Before it was repealed in 1986, the dividend exclusion was set at $200 per couple.

The Bush proposal cuts taxes on dividends. The administration's plan is to exclude dividends from tax at the individual level. They estimate it would save taxpayers a projected $364 billion over the next 10 years. The administration also believes that dividend tax cuts would boost the stock market and reduce incentives for firms to take on too much debt.

(May 2003)

For election, listen to candidate's fiscal-speak

With the Democratic national convention commencing this week, we move into that period of time occurring every four years where political slogans and sound bites rain down—creating the proverbial great flood of ancient times. Insistent campaign promises, ranging from thoughtful to ridiculous will saturate our eyes and ears over the next several months.

While much of the political process is the zealous gathering of support through emotional appeal, there is some quantitative basis underneath these rallying battle cries.

Here's a summary look at the theoretical relationships between government and money.

The government has two major tools for achieving economic health: fiscal policy, through which it determines the appropriate level of taxes and spending; and monetary policy, through which it manages the supply of money.

Since the Depression, the federal government has tried to create a combination of fiscal and monetary policies that will allow sustained growth and stable prices (no inflation).

The primary tools of fiscal policy are spending and taxation. The deliberate manipulation of government purchases, including military (funding a war, for example), public works projects, and scientific research are designed to achieve a balance between full employment, price stability (restrain inflation), and economic growth.

The government has income from only one primary source—taxes. Therefore manipulating tax rates, rules and structures, tax incentives for certain activities (such as investment in long-term assets) are designed to control both the income level of the government and individual disposable income.

The development of fiscal policy is an elaborate process. Each year, the president proposes a budget, or spending plan, to Congress. This is why budget issues are central to a candidate's success. It will be the successful presidential candidate who initiates the government spending process. Virtually every campaign initiative will have an effect on the budget.

Taxation policy affects us more directly. The overall level of taxation is decided through budget negotiations. Although the government ran up deficits, (spending more than it collected in taxes) during the 1970s, '80s, and part of the '90s, the populous generally believe budgets should be balanced.

Historically, most Democrats are willing to tolerate a higher level of taxes to support a more active government, while Republicans generally favor lower taxes and smaller government.

If you keep all this in mind, it will help you to better evaluate campaign promises and proposals.

Although not nearly as emotionally evocative, monetary policy is also central to the government's role in the economic life of the nation. The job of managing the overall economy shifted substantially from fiscal policy to monetary policy during the later years of the 20th century.

The Federal Reserve uses three main devices for maintaining control over the supply of money and credit in the economy: open market operations, the reserve level required by banks, and the discount (interest) rate.

Although not as obvious as interest rates, the most important is open market operations, or the buying and selling of government securities. To increase the supply of money, the Federal Reserve buys government securities from banks, other businesses, or individuals, paying for them with a check or a new source of money that it prints.

Reserve limits for deposit-taking institutions specify how much money is set aside; either as currency in their vaults or deposits at their regional Reserve Bank. Raising reserve requirements forces banks to withhold a larger portion of their funds, thereby reducing the money supply.

The discount rate or interest rate that commercial banks pay to borrow funds from Reserve Banks is by far the most visible tool used in monetary policy. It is the driver that ultimately sets the amount of interest that business and individuals will have to pay when borrowing money. By raising or lowering the discount rate, the Fed can promote or discourage borrowing and thus alter the amount of revenue available to banks for making loans.

Mixing these elements together isn't easy. Additionally, while a strong economy may be a prerequisite to social progress, it may not be the ultimate goal. The traditions of public education, environmental regulations, rules prohibiting discrimination, and government programs like Social Security and Medicare, to name just a few – are also central to American values.

The late U.S. Senator Robert Kennedy explained in 1968 that economic matters are important, but gross national product "does not include the beauty of our poetry or the strength of our marriages; the intelligence of our public debate or the integrity of our public officials. It measures neither our wit nor our courage; neither our wisdom nor our learning; neither our compassion nor our devotion to our country; it measures everything, in short, except that which makes life worthwhile."

(August 2004)

Money matters: You're both a lender, borrower

A recent advertising package from a financial company exhorted the benefits of an "Interest Cancellation Account." The claim was that by becoming involved with their institution, a consumer could "cancel" interest charges on their mortgage.

Using evocative phrases such as, "dramatically reduce interest" and "innovative principles of money management," the company seemed to imply it had discovered some miraculous way to erase most of the cost of borrowing.

The company had built an entire campaign around one of the basic principles of finance—the time value of money. Repay debt more quickly and the interest cost is reduced. Invest money as soon as possible and the total return increases. You don't pay interest on money you don't owe.

As with all financial transactions, there are always two sides—a lender and a borrower. Both are concerned with the time value of money from opposite ends of the spectrum. More importantly, all of us are simultaneously lenders and borrowers affected by time.

The simplest explanation of the time value of money is that a dollar today is worth more than the promise of a dollar tomorrow or at any time in the future, and it's worth less than the dollar you had yesterday.

Part of the reason is daily compounding of interest, but there are other factors affecting why a dollar has different values at different times. Most relate to risk.

Interest is compensation for certain risks, including time. If there's no risk, there's no interest. Therefore, something must be at risk before interest can be "canceled."

You have choices regarding the dollar you have today. You can spend it, invest it or hold it. These choices are opportunity cost. That is, what you don't choose as opposed to what you do choose. Your choices for today's dollar closely relate to time.

If you spend the dollar, you have purchased something you want or need, and you have it now.

If you invest it, it will earn a return and therefore yield more than $1 at some point.

If you hold it, you still have the choice to make in the future, but you have foregone having today whatever you might have purchased, and you have foregone the opportunity to invest it at today's rate, term and type.

The promise of a dollar tomorrow carries some risk, often called the collection risk. You might not get it or get it when promised. Depending on the source of your promised dollar, it may have almost no risk or it may have a high one.

Generally, collection risk increases with time, meaning a dollar owed to you tomorrow has less risk of not being repaid than a dollar owed to you next year. More things can happen to prevent the future payment in the intervening time.

Interest rate risk is also involved in the concept of time value. Market rates fluctuate, and the expectation of whether rates will rise or fall affects loan and investment decisions. If you think that rates are going to increase tomorrow, you could wait to invest that dollar then at a higher rate than you would receive today. If you think rates will decrease, you would invest the dollar today.

Today's dollar, then, has more value than the one you get tomorrow for yet another reason. If rates decrease, not having the dollar today means the opportunity to invest at the higher rate was lost. As with credit risk, the amount of interest rate risk also increases the farther into the future the payment is expected.

Another central factor is inflation. If prices are rising, that dollar in your hand will buy less tomorrow than it will today. This doesn't mean buy everything now. It does need to be considered when making choices about what to do with the dollar and, if it's invested, what return will be needed to keep ahead of rising prices.

Finally, we come to interest and its role. Interest is an incentive to put dollars to work earning money rather than spending it or holding it. Loans are the reverse from the borrower's perspective. The borrower is willing to pay for having the money today.

The interest paid is incentive for the lender to make the funds available as loan funds rather than use the money elsewhere. The interest rate is directly related to each of the risks described above, and results from the fact that money has different value at different times.

The forces of the time value of money are constantly operating. All of us are simultaneous borrows and lenders. Remembering to consider both sides of any time-money situation will lead to clear and understandable fiscal choices.

(July 2005)

RISKS WITH MONEY

There was a time when a fool and his money were soon parted, but now it happens to everybody.

- Adlai Stevenson

Personal use of merchant account comes at a cost

There was once a small business in need of cash. The business had a merchant banking (so it could accept credit cards) account established with a small Oregon bank.

The business owner decided to provide his business some working capital by running his own credit card through the company's merchant banking account. The amount was $4,000. The transaction was rejected.

Why? Because according to the merchant banker, using your personal credit card to fund your own business is illegal by virtue of Federal law-- 16 C.F.R. § 310.3 et. seq.

Is this true? Hardly. But (and it's a big but), *credit card laundering* is a crime. If you have a credit card merchant account for your business and attempt to generate some unrestricted working capital cash by tapping your own credit card, don't do it.

Here are some examples of restrictions on businesses that accept credit cards. Merchants <u>shall</u> <u>not</u>:

- Submit for payment any transaction representing the refinancing of an existing obligation of the cardholder. This includes dishonored checks and charge-backs.

- Allow any other person or business to process transactions through their card terminal.

- Split tickets or process multiple tickets in an effort to gain an authorization for the sale.

- Give a cash refund for a previous credit card sale, but rather shall issue credit on the same credit card.

- Offer cash back on a credit card transaction.
- Under any circumstances, obtain authorization for, nor process sales on any card the Merchant itself is authorized to use. Processing Merchant's own credit card is grounds for immediate termination.

That's the restriction that caused the problem for the proprietor above. The trouble was not the attempt to use personal credit to bolster a young business, but doing it by using a merchant banking relationship in a way that was improper if not illegal.

Notwithstanding abuse of merchant banking relationships, *Inc. Magazine* recently reported that 50 percent of small businesses are financed through personal credit cards. Only 6 percent obtain SBA loans and a mere 2 percent receive funding from venture capital firms.

While credit cards maintain a bit of cultural mystique and magic (generated by the eminence various precious metals), and are extremely convenient to use, they are really nothing more than personally guaranteed lines of credit. Any bank, if inclined, could issue your young business a line of credit; usually under far more favorable terms providing it carries a personal guarantee.

Nevertheless, half the small businesses today use the owner's personal credit cards to finance their growth. The primary stipulation being that the owner doesn't obviously attempt to extract cash from the card into the company's merchant banking account!

As an example, a small manufacturer of furniture found themselves in a market where demand was soaring. With no assets, they used their credit cards for everything from equipment, raw materials, travel expenses and daily operating costs. After six years, the company found that its cost of capital was an overwhelming 23 percent. But profits and volume growth finally did outrun the credit card debt. The obligation was paid off and today the firm has a much more stable capital structure.

One the other hand, the financial landscape is replete with examples of credit card balances becoming so high that monthly debt service (minimum payments) could not be maintained; eventually leading to not just the collapse of the enterprise, but the ruin of personal credit as well.

Credit cards are easy, but expensive and financially brutal.

For most start-ups, there are few friendly financing options. But there are ways to make things easier on yourself if you decide to use personal credit cards.

- Be sure to use different cards for business and personal expenses. The credit card interest on items you charge for your business is tax deductible, personal interest paid is not. Mixing business and personal expenses on the same card inevitably creates confusion and higher exposure on your tax returns.

- Apply for credit cards offered by critical suppliers you use often. Stores such as Staples, Office Depot, and Costco may even issue a card in your business's name.

- Pay your bills promptly with these "private" cards, and it will help you establish a solid credit history as a business; making it easier to graduate to a corporate small-business card, such as those offered by Visa, American Express, and MasterCard.

From there it's just a small step to a truly efficient capital structures and untold fame, wealth and fortune.

But just in case, "don't leave home without it."

(February 2004)

Financial executives can be liable for company misdeeds

If you are the proprietor of a small business (officially a sole proprietorship), there is little or no separation between business and personal money transactions.

If your company borrows money, you have borrowed the money. If your business makes a promise to pay someone, you are automatically personally guaranteeing that payment.

Within corporations however, there is theoretically a shield between the individual and the company when it comes to legal responsibility for financial actions. However, financial executives (and other officers and directors) within corporations are not totally insulated from personal fiscal responsibility.

Corporate liability protection is not unqualified. For example, a corporation cannot:

• Protect you from your own **negligent acts**. Being a director of a corporation does not protect you from personal liability from the wrongs you personally commit. For example: You run a milk delivery service and you fill in for a driver who has called in sick and run into a van full of people; you are personally liable for the damage.

• Protect you from things you **personally guarantee**. Banks and corporate creditors often require personal guarantees from people in a corporation. If your business fails, you are personally responsible for repaying these debts.

• Protect you from personally paying **governmental employment withholding taxes and sales taxes**. When taxes are held in trust, all officers and anyone who has <u>check-signing authority</u> are jointly liable to the government for these taxes. That means that as a principal, you cannot hide behind the corporation and will be personally liable for these taxes if they are not paid.

- Protect you from personally liability for **unpaid employee wages**. In some states, this extends to the ten largest shareholders as well. Until this past February, Colorado had this personal liability provision. However, recently it was removed by the Colorado Supreme Court in the Leonard v. McMorris case.

Another area of personal exposure is the *Alter-ego Doctrine*. Under this doctrine, when a corporate entity is used to perpetuate a fraud, circumvent a statute, or accomplish some other wrongful or inequitable purpose, the courts may not observe the separation of corporation and its stockholders. Unfortunately, this doctrine only comes into play when unscrupulous people are attempting to extract money for their own personal pleasure. Note that this doctrine extends to shareholders as well as officers and directors.

In the early years of a company's life, almost all participants are involved in raising money. Amidst all the excitement of a new venture, it's very important to remember that simply forming a corporation does not protect its officers and directors from fraud; particularly securities fraud.

Officers and directors face personal liability under a collection of provisions in the Securities Act of 1933 and 1934. Violations of various sections (and rules relating to) the 1933 and 1934 Act may subject directors to personal liability for making false or misleading statements or omitting material information in documents that are filed with the SEC.

Finally, directors may be held liable for violations of Rule 10b-5 of the 1934 Act. This rule forbids anyone with material nonpublic information about a security from conducting transactions on the basis of that nonpublic information. Insider trading and tipping by a director can result in the forfeiture of any profits by the insider, heavy civil penalties, and criminal prosecution. The most notorious insider traders have been rewarded with lengthy prison terms.

Two recent specific examples (with names omitted to protect the guilty) of fraud cases include:

- Overstating advertising revenues by $46 million (64%) for the first three quarters of 2001. The defendants each agreed to settle the Commission's lawsuit, and to plead guilty to the criminal charges.
- Improper and misleading accounting and deceptive disclosures relating to a $300 million financing transaction.

All of the above is a rather long-winded way of saying, "Don't lie, either by construction or omission."

If you deal with money, particularly within a corporation here are "seven habits of highly effective people" that are not in jail.

- Tell the truth.
- Don't write checks until your deposit has cleared the bank.
- Disclose to your stockholders the truth about today, leave personal prognostications at the office.
- Pay your employees what you owe them.
- Don't do anything that requires you to "fix it later."
- Don't borrow money personally from your company.

- Don't gossip over martinis about your publicly traded company.

Taking these habits to heart would certainly change the recent headlines regarding officer wrongdoings from visions of horizontal stripes to more vertical views of fiscal prosperity.

(October 2003)

Federal Reserve handles more than just interest rates

The recent nomination of Ben Bernanke to succeed Alan Greenspan as chairman of the Federal Reserve Board has brought renewed attention to our banking system and monetary policy. The chairman's job often is described as the second most-powerful one in the nation.

The chairman has the responsibility to oversee the Board's implementation of the Federal Reserve Act. The act came into being in 1913, and established the Federal Reserve System and other laws pertaining to a wide range of banking and financial activities.

The board's most well-known activity is adjustment to the Fed Funds Rate—the interest rate at which banks lend to each other overnight. This interest rate is considered to be the "rate within the rate," theoretically the risk-free rate upon which all other lending rates are based.

However, in addition to the widely visible adjustments to the Fed Funds Rate, the Federal Reserve Board (already being dubbed "Bernanke's Board") also has responsibility to oversee and manage 31 other components of the country's banking and financial systems. The details of these areas can be found in Title 12, Chapter II, 201, et. seq., of the Code of Federal Regulations (CFR).

Here's a look a some of the less visible, but just as significant, activities of the Federal Reserve Board.

The first four areas of regulation directly affect fairness and seek to maintain integrity within the banking system.

- Equal credit opportunity: Prohibits lenders from discriminating against credit applicants, establishes guidelines for gathering and evaluating credit information, and requires written notification when credit is denied. Civil rights (including fiscal rights) require constant attention, especially in the area of gender and age.
- Home mortgage disclosure: Requires certain mortgage lenders to disclose data regarding their lending patterns. This is a particularly critical area because historically low interest rates have fueled increased, sometimes unscrupulous, mortgage lending activities.
- Truth in lending: Prescribes uniform methods for computing the cost of credit, disclosing credit terms and resolving errors on certain types of credit accounts.
- Unfair or deceptive acts or practices: Establishes consumer complaint procedures and defines unfair or deceptive practices in extending credit to consumers. It's related to the disclosure requirements above and designed to ensure integrity in the lending process.

The next three components are exceptionally essential as we carry out more business through electronic mechanisms. Transferring funds between entities is one thing. Ensuring the availability of those funds remains a problematic issue for banking intermediaries.

- Electronic fund transfers: Establishes the rights, liabilities, and responsibilities of parties in electronic funds transfers and protects consumers when they use such systems.
- Collection of checks and other items: Establishes procedures, duties, and responsibilities among Federal Reserve Banks, the senders and payers

of checks and other items, and the senders and recipients of Fed wire funds transfers.

- Availability of funds and collection of checks: Governs the availability of funds deposited in checking accounts, and the collection and return of checks. This is frequently a controversial area because honest funds should be available immediately; however, banks must still protect themselves from fraud.

- Loans to executive officers, directors, and principal shareholders of member banks: Restricts credit that a member bank may extend to its executive officers, directors, and principal shareholders and their related interests. This is another example of enlarged corporate governance.

- Credit by banks for the purpose of purchasing or carrying margin stocks: Governs extension of credit by banks or persons other than brokers or dealers to finance the purchase or the carrying of margin securities.

- Bank holding companies and change in bank control: Regulates the acquisition and control of banks, defines and regulates the nonbanking activities that banks within the United States may engage in, and establishes the minimum ratios of capital to assets that bank holding companies must maintain.

In addition to providing antitrust and collusion protection, this regulation controls the relative aggressiveness of the lending market.

- Obtaining and using medical information in connection with credit: Interim rules creating exceptions to the statutory prohibition against obtaining or using medical information in connection with determining eligibility for credit.

This new regulation will be effective March 7, 2006, and contains many complex civil, and interlocking fiscal issues.

The non-interest-rate management activities of the Federal Reserve Board can have considerable effects on individuals and business, from civil rights to protection from fraud.

For the most current activities of the Federal Reserve Board under its new chairman, and any other changes to the CFR, you may monitor the Electronic Code of Federal Regulations (e-CFR) through the Web site ecfr.gpoaccess.gov.

The e-CFR prototype is a demonstration project. It's not an official legal edition of the CFR. The official code may be found at:
www.gpoaccess.gov/cfr/index.html.

(November 2005)

Regulation allows creditors access to medical records

The last time you applied for a loan, the fact you had measles at age 9 probably didn't enter your mind. Likewise, the application didn't ask about your plans to repair that pesky left knee meniscus tear.

Nevertheless, a new federal rule that went into effect April 1—Regulation FF—grants exceptions that allow creditors to obtain or use medical information for determining credit-worthiness. Although limited to circumstances that creditors believe are "necessary and appropriate," they may use certain health information as part of their evaluation process.

Also, the rule allows creditors to share medical information with affiliates in certain situations.

The Fair Credit Reporting Act (FCRA), defines "medical information" as information or data, whether oral or recorded, in any form or medium, created by or derived from a health care provider or the consumer that relates to (1) the past, present, or future physical, mental, or behavioral health or condition of an individual; (2) health care provided to an individual; or (3) the payment for the provision of health care to an individual.

Under the FCRA, "medical information" doesn't include:

- Age or gender of the consumer.
- Demographic information about the consumer.
- Any other information about a consumer that doesn't relate to the physical, mental, or behavioral health or condition of a consumer, including the existence or value of an insurance policy.

Under Regulation FF, it's acceptable for a creditor to receive unsolicited medical information. However, the creditor may use that information only to the extent provided by the exceptions in the regulation.

The "financial information exception" contains a three-part test:

- The information must be the type routinely used in making credit eligibility determinations.
- The creditor must use the information in a manner and to an extent no less favorable than it would use comparable non-medical information in a credit transaction.
- The creditor must not take the consumer's physical, mental, or behavioral health, condition or history, type of treatment or prognosis into account as part of any such determination of credit eligibility.

This test is intended to balance creditors' obtaining and using certain medical information about consumers when necessary and appropriate to satisfy prudent underwriting criteria (ensuring that credit is extended in a safe and sound matter), while at the same time restricting the use of medical information for inappropriate purposes.

Given that information tends to develop wings of its own, the rule specifies that medical information may be shared with affiliates if:

(1) The information is shared in connection with the business of insurance or annuities.

(2) For any purpose permitted without authorization under the Health Insurance Portability and Accountability Act (HIPAA).

(3) For any purpose referred to in Section 1179 of HIPAA.

(4) For any purpose described in Section 502(e) of the Gramm-Leach-Bliley Act.

Nevertheless, now that these rules are in effect, borrowers may wish to monitor not just their credit bureau scores, but medical records as well. Not surprisingly, there's an organization that collects, monitors, and provides such information—The Medical Information Bureau (MIB).

The MIB will provide consumers a disclosure once annually without charge. To obtain this free disclosure, call MIB's toll-free phone number, 866-692-6901.

You'll be asked to certify, under penalty of perjury, that the information you provide about yourself to request an MIB disclosure is accurate, complete, and that you're the person requesting disclosure. If you haven't applied for individually underwritten life, health or disability insurance during the preceding seven-year period, MIB may not have a record on you.

Many people consider information about their health to be highly sensitive, deserving of the strongest protection under the law. Long-standing laws in many states and the age-old tradition of doctor-patient privilege have been the mainstay of privacy protection for decades.

HIPAA is designed to protect the appropriate use of medical information. An organization called the Privacy Rights Clearinghouse provides useful information.

For more official information regarding the privacy of your personal information, you may wish to explore the U.S. Department of Health and Human Services, Office of Civil Rights, 200 Independence Avenue, S.W., Washington, D.C. 20201; phone, 866-627-7748 and Web site, **www.hhs.gov.**

Also, contact the U.S. Department of Labor regarding privacy of medical information in the workplace, including your employer's health and safety files and family-leave records. Contact info is U.S. Department of Labor, 200 Constitution Ave., NW, Washington, DC 20210; phone, 866-487-2365 and Web site, **www.dol.gov**.

Web links to the 50 states' DOL offices may be found at **www.dol.gov/esa/contacts/state_of.htm**.

Contact the Federal Trade Commission to learn about health information collected for employment background checks at:
www.ftc.gov/bcp/conline/pubs/buspubs/credempl.

Find applications for insurance coverage at:
www.ftc.gov/bcp/conline/pubs/buspubs/insurers/.

(April 2006)

Options are scandal from ghosts of Christmas past, future

The holidays have arrived. As the seasonal song says, "He's making a list, checking it twice. Gonna find out who's naughty and nice."

Once again, Santa Claus is shaking his head at the financial community. If this keeps up, Santa's annual trip will be so short, he'll need only four reindeer.

This year, the activities that are increasing the "naughty" list have been dubbed, "The Options Scandal." According to Forbes, as of October, more than 150 companies have been engulfed in this embarrassment and embezzlement.

Let's examine the nature of "options" and the source of this scandal.

An option is a contract that gives the buyer the right, but not the obligation, to buy or sell an underlying asset at a specified price on or before a specified date. An option is a binding contract with strictly defined terms and properties.

Since option contracts can be for either a sale or a purchase, the idea was originally to protect, or hedge, an investment. Additionally, many companies use employee stock option plans to compensate, retain and attract employees. These plans are contracts that give employees the right to buy the company's shares at a fixed price within a certain period of time. They hope to profit by exercising their options in the future at a higher price than when they were granted.

If you're a shareholder in a public company, watch for SEC filings of Form S-8 and Form 4. This may tell you the firm is using options as compensation, thereby eroding the value of the stock in general.

The two types of options are "calls" and "puts." A call gives the holder the right to buy an asset at a certain price within a specific period of time. Buyers of calls hope that the stock will increase substantially before the option expires.

A put gives the holder the right to sell an asset at a certain price within a specific period of time. Buyers of puts hope that the price of the stock will fall before the option expires.

If you already own the asset for which you're purchasing an option, it's called a "covered" option. Trading in just the options alone, without owning the underlying security, is known as an uncovered or "naked" option.

The current options scandal has to do with time. An option contract is for a specific period of time from the date it was granted. Under fair and legal rules, after making a considered prediction about which way the price will move, people buy options and hope they've accurately predicted the future.

However, in the current cases, options were executed today for a date in the past at a price that the issuer and buyer already knew was lower than today's worth. It's just like betting on a football game where you already know the results.

Is this a new high-tech scheme? Hardly. It's the oldest scheme in the books, made even more famous in the movie "The Sting" where the entire scheme was based on the practice of "past posting."

Past posting is simply making a bet on a known outcome. This is possibly the best-known con trick of all time. A close cousin to the current scandal involving past-posting options is insider trading. Illegal insider trading would occur if the CEO of Company A learned (prior to a public announcement) that Company

A will be taken over, and bought shares in Company A knowing the share price likely would rise.

One of the strangest cases occurred at Cablevision (NYSE: CVC), which announced late in September that it had granted stock options to a dead executive and then backdated the award to when he was alive.

Backdating options isn't just a one- or two-person scam. It affects every shareholder of the firm. The deception manipulates financial statements—increasing profits, lowering taxes and affecting the overall stock price.

Options are supposed to be managed by the compensation committee of the board of directors. Recent research has discovered common board members across several companies involved in the swindle.

For example, VeriSign has other directors with ties to more than one company in the scandal, including Roger Moore of Western Digital Corp. and Gregory Reyes, the former CEO of San Jose-based Brocade Communications System Inc. Reyes became the first prominent Silicon Valley leader to face criminal charges in the options mess.

Maybe we should borrow another few lines from the holiday carol:

"He sees you when you're sleeping. He knows when you're awake. He knows if you've been bad or good. So be good for goodness' sake."

(December 2006)

PLAYING WITH MONEY

Not only do the children enjoy these games, which involve buying and selling with play money, but they learn an essential ingredient of motivation in our society: greed.

- William E Bill Vaughan
(American Writer, b. 1915)

Derivatives – aka 'synthetic securities' – are worth a look

Headlines in the financial press often include the word "derivatives," usually associated with a problem, loss or conflict. But, what are derivatives? How are they used? Why are these securities so often the object of derision?

Following is a brief exploration of derivatives, aka synthetic securities.

Derivatives began as the combination of an asset with an agreement to buy or sell that asset as a specified price. Thus the term "synthetic security." The intent was to limit (or transfer) the risk of loss.

The transfer of risk is accomplished through the use of option or futures contracts. Due to the number of possible combinations, options and futures contracts can be a bit mystifying and complicated at first. Yet they are nothing more than either a promise to buy or a promise to sell. These promises to buy or sell are linked to everything from specific commodities (orange juice or sugar) to the stock market and money itself. Options and futures contracts may also apply to overall market indices such as the S&P 500 or Dow Jones Industrial Average.

A basic example is: an investor owns XYZ security purchased for $100. While holding that security, the investor assumes all of the risk of the price either rising or falling. Theoretically, the risk of loss is $100 and the reward is unlimited. If this risk is too large, the investor also enters into an agreement to sell XYZ security at $80 anytime within the next 12 months.

The combination of these two securities creates a synthetic investment with a guaranteed loss limit of

$20, hence a derivative. The fees associated with entering into the options contract is the premium for this risk of loss insurance.

Since 1977 when the Chicago Board of Trade introduced a futures contract based on the U.S. 20-year bond, the market for derivative securities has become very large. Worldwide, these securities provide "insurance" on an estimated $16 trillion of financial instruments. Their economic function is to transfer risk from those who do not want to bear it to those who are willing to bear it for a fee.

Derivatives are also commonly used by companies involved in international trade. Fluctuations in currency exchange rates represent a high degree of risk.

The most active derivatives in currencies include: Deutschemark/dollar; Japanese Yen/dollar; Swiss Franc/dollar; British Pound/dollar; French Franc/dollar. As a further hedge against international volatility, international equity indices are also used to create derivative securities that limit risk. Examples include: the S&P 500 Index (U.S.A.); Nikkei 225 Index (Japan); CAC 40 Index (France); FTSE-100 index (UK); DAX Index (Germany).

Creating a derivative security based upon an instrument the investor already owns is called "hedging." Hedgers are farmers, manufacturers, importers and exporters, and securities investors. A hedger buys or sells in the futures markets to secure the future price of a commodity intended to be sold at a later date. This helps protect against price decrease.

Entering into options or futures contracts (sometimes more than one at a time) without owning the underlying security is referred to "speculation," or "being naked."

Speculators do not aim to minimize risk but rather to benefit from the inherently risky nature of the futures market. Speculators aspire to profit from the price change that hedgers are protecting themselves against. In other words, rather than transferring existing risk, the speculator hopes that the hedging activities of others will increase the price of the option or futures contract for themselves.

This is the cause of the negativity and disapproval regarding derivatives. As hedging activities within companies increase and become more intricate, the risk of loss rises. Firms may unintentionally find themselves speculating rather than hedging simply because of multifarious positions created by simultaneous derivative positions. Another factor may be the lure of excess profits from speculating on top of an existing hedging activity.

In March 2004, it was reported that Fannie Mae paid a net $25.1 billion for derivatives transactions in fewer than four years—nearly all of which may represent losses that cannot be recouped. Gibson Greetings and Proctor & Gamble lost $20 million and $157 million respectively from derivative transactions.

In response to rising concerns that derivatives were undermining the basic efficiency and stability of financial markets, The Financial Economists Roundtable concluded that derivatives serve a highly useful risk-management role for both financial and non-financial firms.

Although some major derivative users, mutual funds, hedge funds, securities firms, and even banks have incurred derivatives-related losses, most of these losses have been due to inadequate risk-management systems and poor operations control and supervision.

However, these losses have not threatened the overall stability and efficiency of financial markets. The best discipline against risk in any market, including derivatives, is to ensure that participants have an incentive to manage themselves prudently.

(March 2005)

Arbitrage can be lucrative, but be real careful about timing

The R&B singer Billy Preston pined in 1974, "Nothin' from nothin' leaves nothin'. You gotta bring me somethin' if you wanna be with me."

If a person wanted to bring Billy "something," but had "nothing," what could they do? Where do any of us turn when we crave "something from nothing?"

The answer? Arbitrage!

Arbitrage is defined to be the simultaneous purchase and sale of a security (or anything else for that matter) in order to profit from a <u>difference</u> in the price. This usually takes place on separate exchanges or marketplaces.

For example, if the price of a stock on the New York Stock Exchange is $10 per share, but on the Frankfurt exchange, $8 per share, the $2 difference could be an immediate profit requiring zero investment. Here's how it would work.

The "Arbitrageur" sells on the New York exchange while simultaneously buying on the Frankfurt exchange. Since the transactions are theoretically simultaneous, there is an immediate gain of $2 per share.

Furthermore, since the gain is guaranteed by the disparity in price, there is no limit (except total shares issued and available for trading) on the number of shares that could be bought and sold. A 100 million share purchase, coupled with a simultaneous 100 million share sale, nets the arbitrageur a quick $200 million.

The concept of arbitrage is not limited to financial instruments. The procedure could be applied to any situation where there is an immediate opportunity to buy and sell concurrently at different prices. It even can even happen on eBay.

For example, Wal-Mart is selling the DVD of *Barbarella* for $10.

However, the last copies of *Barbarella* on eBay have sold for an average of $25. The arbitrageur buys copies of the movie at $10 from Wal-Mart and sells them on eBay for an almost instant profit of $15. .

But, this will not continue for long, as one of three things (the application of the "Efficient Market Hypothesis") should happen.

- Wal-Mart runs out of copies of *Barbarella* on DVD.

- Wal-Mart raises the price on the remaining copies as they've seen an increased demand for the movie.

- The supply of *Barbarella* DVDs skyrockets on eBay, which causes the price to fall.

This kind of arbitrage is quite common. Many eBay sellers will go to flea markets and yard sales looking for collectibles that the seller does not know the true value of and has priced much too low. For instance, buying rare collections of video games for $10 then selling them on eBay for $100

This example is not quite pure arbitrage because it requires a small amount of "something" to establish the initial inventory. Moreover as the example above shows, as more information enters the marketplace (both at Wal-Mart and eBay); the price difference will close and become equal.

This equalization is known as an "efficient" market. In an efficient market, all information is known across all trading places. With a sufficient number of participants buying and selling, prices will equalize making pure arbitrage impossible. Timing is critical.

One of the most alluring and active areas of arbitrage is currency exchange; particularly cross-currency arbitrage. This usually involves complex mathematics, such as matrix algebra, and the ability to execute trades quickly before the disparity is discovered.

For example, while traveling in Europe we discover that, given certain circumstances, we can exchange dollars for francs, francs for pounds, pounds for deutsche marks, and finally the deutsche marks for the original dollars spawning a small profit.

Using elementary matrix algebra searching for an unbalanced matrix, we can instantly identify a profitable currency arbitrage opportunity.

Without recounting all the intricate details of the calculations here, suffice it to say that with a PC and real-time currency data feeds, it's easy to create hundreds of matrices—each containing a different set of exchange rates. The system could then automatically alert the user of temporary currency exchange imbalances that could be exploited before economic forces restore equilibrium.

For those interested in exploring cross-currency arbitrage more closely, visit the following websites:

www.3d2f.com,
www.finaldownload.com,
www.888options.com, and
www.tradelikethepros.com.

If all this is beginning to sound too complicated, there's more.

Consider arbitrage as it relates to derivatives. In this case, synthetic securities are created by combining an asset with one or more options or futures contracts.

This hybrid-security is then used as a basis for searching out other single or combined securities for an arbitrage trade.

Timing is everything. The forces of the efficient market hypothesis generally close arbitrage windows of opportunity very quickly.

Another important factor is transaction coats. The fees charged by brokers to execute the trades must be considered in the calculations. In other words, the price difference must be large enough to cover the broker's charges.

There may be no such thing as a free lunch, but arbitrage remains an attractive buffet.

(April 2005)

Hedge fund managers can employ numerous strategies

In recent months, the term "hedge fund manager" appeared frequently in the press—usually in combination with the words "fraud," "conflict of interest," and "crime."

Before you begin to wonder how someone who manages "a fence or boundary formed by a dense row of shrubs or low trees" could commit fraud, let's examine the definition of "hedge" as it applies to finance.

In finance, hedge means making an investment to reduce the risk of adverse price movements in an asset, usually through an offsetting position in a related security.

Hedge funds aren't the same as mutual funds. Hedge funds are far more capricious in their investment options. They can use short selling, leverage, derivatives, put and call options, futures contracts, and more. The hedge fund manager creates a far more complex and free-ranging set of financial instruments than mutual funds.

Hedge fund strategies attempt to be unaffected by the direction of the bond (debt) or equity (stock) markets—unlike conventional equity or mutual funds, which generally accept 100 percent of market risk. That is, the hedge fund is a "boundary" against market volatility.

Hedge funds are estimated to be a $1.1 trillion industry and growing every year, with approximately 9,000 distinct funds. Most of these funds are highly specialized, relying on the specific expertise of the manager.

In general, long-term hedge fund returns have outperformed standard equity and bond indexes with less volatility and less risk of loss than stocks.

Sophisticated investors, including many Swiss and other private banks—that have lived through, and understand the consequences of, major stock market corrections—favor participating in hedge funds. Endowments and pension funds also allocate assets to hedge funds.

Hedge fund managers employ 12 fundamental strategies. Here's an overview of each approach.

- **Universal-** Aims to profit from changes in global economies, typically brought about by shifts in government policy that affect interest rates, in turn affecting currency, stock and bond markets.

- **Arbitrage-** Attempts to remove most market risk by taking offsetting positions, often in different securities of the same issuer. May also use futures to limit interest-rate risk.

- **Short selling-** Sells securities (before buying them) in anticipation of falling prices and being able to re-buy them at a future date. Often used as a hedge to offset long-only portfolios and by those who feel the market is approaching a declining cycle.

- **Opportunity event-** Profits arise from events such as IPOs, sudden price changes often caused by an interim earnings disappointment, hostile bids and other actions.

- **Multi-strategy-** The manager employs various strategies simultaneously to realize short- and long-term gains. This style of investing allows the manager to combine different strategies to capitalize on current investment opportunities.

- **Special situation-** Invests in event-driven situations such as mergers, hostile takeovers, reorganizations or leveraged buyouts. May involve simultaneous purchase of stock in companies being acquired, and the sale of stock in its acquirer, hoping to profit from the spread.

- **Value discount-** Purchases securities perceived to be selling at deep discounts to their intrinsic or potential worth. Such securities may also be out of favor with analysts.
- **Aggressive growth-** Invests in equities expected to experience accelerated earnings per share growth. Generally high price/earnings ratios, low or no dividends; often smaller and micro-cap stocks that are expected to experience rapid growth.
- **Distressed-** Acquires equity and debt at deep discounts of companies in or facing bankruptcy or reorganization. Profits derive from the market's lack of understanding of the true value of deeply discounted securities.
- **Emerging markets-** Invests in equity or debt of emerging markets that tend to have high and volatile growth.
- **Fund of funds-** Mixes and matches hedge funds and other pooled investment vehicles. Returns, risk and volatility are controlled by the blend of underlying strategies and funds. Capital preservation is generally an important consideration.
- **Income-** Invests with primary focus on yield or current income rather than solely on capital gains.

With all the freedom and complexity involved in hedge fund management, it's not hard to imagine how fraud and conflict of interest can arise.

In May 2006, Patrick Parkinson of the Federal Reserve testified, "Hedge funds clearly are becoming more important in the capital markets as sources of liquidity and holders and managers of risk. But as their importance has grown, so too have concerns about investor protection and systemic risk.

"The SEC believes that the examination of registered hedge advisers will deter fraud. But investors must not view SEC regulation of advisers as an effective substitute for their own due diligence in selecting funds and their own monitoring of hedge fund performance."

(September 2006)

WATCHING THE MONEY

Do not be fooled into believing that because a man is rich he is necessarily smart. There is ample proof to the contrary.
- Julius Rosenwald, *US merchant & philanthropist (1862 – 1932)*

Ah Spring! When a young man's fancy turns to . . .
bond ratings?

"In the spring a young man's fancy lightly turns to thoughts of love." This line is from the poem, "Locksley Hall," by Alfred, Lord Tennyson. However, spring also brings thoughts of other things—like how, after paying all those taxes last month, can we make more money than last year?

One way is to pay more attention to the credit rating of companies in which we invest. In financial circles "AAA" does not mean American Automobile Association. Likewise, "CC" does not stand for "Carbon Copy."

Here's a brief look at those ratings; where they come from, and what they mean.

Over one hundred years ago, after Moody was wiped out in the 1907 stock market crash, he came back with an idea: this time an analysis of security values for investors. Thus was born Moody's Investors Service, the world's largest rating agency, which now has more than 700 analysts working in 14 countries.

Standard & Poor's, a division of The McGraw-Hill Companies, was established in 1860, to provide independent insight, analysis, and information to the financial community. Along with Moody's, Standard & Poor's is a pre-eminent global provider of independent financial analysis and information.

Moody's and S&P's dominate the US market, where ratings have for decades been vital tools for issuers and investors. But, with the advent of the Euro bond market, European investors are becoming more rating conscious.

Ratings are basically tools for differentiating credit quality. Standard & Poor's defines a *rating* as an "opinion on the general creditworthiness of an obligor." The rating process includes quantitative, qualitative and legal analysis.

Moody's long-term rating definitions range from Aaa to C, or from golden-edged bonds to those having extremely poor prospects of ever attaining any solid investment standing. On this scale, any bonds below Ba generally lack characteristics of a desirable investment.

Rating is largely what determines the borrower's ability to raise money by issuing debt (Bonds) on favorable terms.

The actual ratings definitions are:

Moody's Long-Term Debt Ratings

- Aaa - Best quality. Smallest degree of risk. "Gilt edged." Interest payments protected by a large or very stable margin and principal is secure.

- Aa - Of high quality by all standards. Margins of protection may not be as large as Aaa or fluctuation of protective elements may be of greater amplitude.

- A - Many favorable attributes; upper-medium-grade obligations. Security considered adequate, but may be susceptible to impairment in the future.

- Baa - Medium-grade obligations neither highly protected nor poorly secured. Security appears adequate at present but certain protective elements may be unreliable over any great length of time. Speculative characteristics.

- Ba - Judged to have speculative elements; future cannot be considered as well-assured. The protection of interest and principal payments may be very moderate and not well safeguarded during both good and bad times.

- B - Generally lacks characteristics of a desirable investment. Assurance of interest and principal payments or of maintenance of other terms of the contract over any long period of time may be small.
- Caa - Of poor standing. Such issues may be in default or there may be present elements of danger with respect to principal or interest.
- Ca - Speculative in a high degree. Such issues are often in default or have other marked shortcomings.
- C - Extremely poor prospects of ever attaining any real investment standing.

Standard & Poor's Long-Term Issuer Credit Ratings

- AAA - Extremely strong capacity to meet its financial commitments. The highest Issuer Credit Rating assigned by Standard & Poor's.
- AA - Very strong capacity to meet its financial commitments. It differs from the highest rated obligors only in small degree.
- A - Strong capacity to meet its financial commitments but is somewhat more susceptible to changes in circumstances.
- BBB - Adequate capacity to meet its financial commitments. However, adverse economic conditions or changing circumstances are more likely to lead to a weakened capacity to meet its financial commitments.
- BB, B, CCC, and CC ratings have significant speculative characteristics. BB is less vulnerable near term but faces major uncertainties; adverse conditions could lead to inadequate capacity to meet commitments.
- B - More vulnerable than obligors rated BB, but currently has the capacity to meet financial commitments. Adverse conditions will likely impair

the obligor's capacity or willingness to meet its financial commitments.

- CCC - Currently vulnerable and is dependent upon favorable business, financial, and economic conditions to meet financial commitments.
- CC - Currently highly vulnerable.

To paraphrase a well-known love-song, "just remember in the winter, far beneath the bitter snow, lies the 'CC,' that with careful analysis, in the spring becomes the AAA."

(May 2004)

Performance indicators can be guide to future numbers

Most of us are familiar with economic and financial indexes (or indices). We hear daily reports of the change in "The Dow Jones Industrial Average," or the "Standard and Poor's 500." These measurements are designed to provide indications of performance for the group of securities or activities (such as consumer spending) they represent.

In general, an index is a statistical indicator providing a representation of the value of the securities (or activities) which constitute it. Indexes often serve as barometers for a given market or industry and provide benchmarks against which financial or economic performance is measured.

An index itself merely reports what happened. Nevertheless, based upon the tenuous assumption that the markets have memory, investors seek to uncover underlying relationships that can be used predict the future.

When researching or monitoring a stock, bond, or mutual fund, indexes similar to the investment will reveal how its performance compares to similar investments. For stocks and bonds, the most common investment indexes are:

- Dow Jones Industrial Average: 30 U.S. "Blue Chip" stocks. Much of the public keeps track how the market is performing by this yardstick.
- Standard and Poor's (S&P) 500: 500 large, domestic stocks.
- Wilshire 5000: The entire U.S. stock market. This is the most comprehensive domestic index.

- Russell 3000: Stocks of 3,000 of the largest U.S. corporations.
- Morgan Stanley Europe and Far East: The world's major non-U.S. stock markets.
- Lehman Brothers Government Bond Index: U.S. government agency and Treasury bonds.
- Lehman Brothers Corporate Bond Index: Investment-grade corporate bonds.

However, given the relatively stagnant performance of the economy over the last several years, other indexes are receiving more attention; attempting to segregate and reveal information that would lead to prospective profit. Many investors are sharpening their look into the markets based upon geography or industry.

Here are some of the indexes that reflect this more focused look into investing behavior:

- NASDAQ Biotechnology Index: The NASDAQ Biotechnology Index contains companies that are classified according to the Financial Times and the London Stock Exchange ("FTSE") Global Classification System as either biotechnology or pharmaceutical which also meet other eligibility criteria.
- NASDAQ Computer Index: The NASDAQ Computer Index contains NASDAQ listed companies classified as Computer Hardware, Semiconductors, and Software & Computer Services, including firms that manufacture and distribute computers and associated electronic data processing equipment and accessories, semiconductor capital equipment, manufacturers and distributors of wafers and chips, providers of computer services and IT consultants, internet access providers,

internet software and on-line service providers, and producers and distributors of computer software.

- Gold BUGS Index (HUI): An acronym for **B**asket of **U**nhedged **G**old **S**tocks, the BUGS index is made up exclusively of mining stocks that do not hedge their gold positions more than a year-and-a-half into the future. When gold prices are on the rise, the Gold BUGS Index provides an excellent way for investors to capitalize on that increase. The index has a high correlation to the spot price (current price) of gold.

- S&P SmallCap 600: The S&P SmallCap 600 Index invests in a basket of small-cap equities. A small-cap company is generally defined as a stock with a market capitalization between $300 million and $2 billion.

- International indexes include the following major exchange indexes:

- FTSE Index - The Financial Times 100 Index, or FTSE, reports the performance of equities traded on the London Stock Exchange.

- Bovespa Index - tracks the performance of a basket of stocks that trade on the Sao Paulo Exchange.

- DAX Index - the most commonly cited benchmark for measuring the returns posted by stocks on the Frankfurt Stock Exchange.

- CAC-40 Index - the benchmark tracking index for the Paris Bourse.

- Hang Seng Index - the leading index for shares traded on the Hong Kong Stock Exchange.

- Straits Times Index - compiled by the newspaper of the same name, is Singapore's premier equity index.

- KOSPI Index - In South Korea, the main tracking index is the Korean Composite Stock Price Index, or KOSPI for short.

One last specialized index is of note. The Domini 400 Social Index. This index is a market capitalization-weighted common stock index. It monitors the performance of 400 U.S. corporations that pass multiple, broad-based social and ethical screens. The index contains 250 companies from Standard & Poor's 500 Index, 100 additional large companies not included in the S&P 500 but providing industry representation, and approximately 50 additional companies with particularly strong social characteristics.

As you search for potential investments, make sure to use the appropriate market index for your particular target. Market indexes are useful tools for the trader but should never be used in isolation from other market factors.

(September 2005)

Financial planning resources are easy to find

How many times have we heard (or said), "If you're so smart, why aren't you rich?"

Whether it's from a scholarly paper with the subtitle "an analysis of the asymptotic properties of Pareto optimal consumption allocations in a stochastic general equilibrium model with heterogeneous consumers," or from the 1992 episode of "Batman" with the same title, somehow the connection between intelligence and wealth seems to make sense.

It probably would be bad form to ask someone who's very wealthy, "If you're so rich, why aren't you smart?"

So where can we turn to test our personal store of smarts related to investing? Here are some readily accessible resources for building investment intelligence.

▪ The Securities and Exchange Commission provides a number of tools for investors. A helpful real-time quiz appears on the Web at **www.sec.gov/investor/tools/quiz.htm**. It's a 10-question multiple-choice quiz that provides explanations for each answer.

For example, "Over the past 70 years, the type of investment that has earned the most money, or the highest rate of return, for investors has been A. Stocks, B. Corporate Bonds, C. Savings accounts, D. Don't know."

Answer: A. Stocks.

If you had invested $1 in the stocks of large companies in 1925 and re-invested all dividends, your dollar would be worth $2,350 at the end of 1998. If the same dollar had been invested in corporate bonds, it would be worth $61, and in U.S. Treasury bills, it would be worth $15.

Another example is the explanation of stocks vs. bonds. When you buy a bond, you're lending money to the company. The company promises to pay you interest and to return your money on a specific date. This promise generally makes bonds safer than stocks, but bonds can be risky. Unlike stockholders, bond-holders know how much money they will make, unless the company goes out of business.

When you own stock, you own a part of the company. There are no guarantees of profits, or even that you'll get your original investment back, but you might make money in two ways.

First, the stock price can rise if the company does well and other investors want to buy the stock. If a stock's price rises from $10 to $12, the $2 increase is called a "capital gain" or "appreciation."

Second, a company sometimes pays out a part of its profits to stockholders—that's called a "dividend."

An even more detailed resource is provided by the National Association of Securities Dealers (NASD) on its web site at

apps.nasd.com/Investor_Information/quiz/.

One quiz question: If a company files for bankruptcy, which of the following securities is most at risk of becoming worthless?

Answer: Among those with claims to a bankrupt company's assets, shareholders of common stock have the last claim on any assets, falling in line behind secured creditors, bondholders, and owners of preferred shares. Common shareholders may not receive anything if the secured and unsecured creditors' claims aren't fully repaid.

Another example is, which is the best definition of "selling short?" Answer: Short selling involves borrowing stock from a broker through a margin account and selling it, with the understanding that it must later be bought back and returned to the broker.

If the stock declines in value, as the short seller hopes, the investor will profit since the value of the stock borrowed and sold would be higher than the stock subsequently purchased and returned to the broker. However, if the stock rises in value, the investor must pay the difference to make good on the stock owed to the broker.

The NASD also provides useful calculators to help us with our arithmetic intelligence. The website, **www.nasd.com/InvestorInformation/ToolsCalculators/**, the online tools and calculators include:

- Analyze mutual-fund and ETF fees and expenses
  - Look up mutual-fund breakpoint information
  - Retirement calculator
  - College calculator
  - Investor knowledge quiz
  - Loan calculator
  - Savings calculator
  - Kids' calculator
  - Saving for my summer vacation
  - The Stock Market Game
  - Minimum required distribution calculator
  - Accrued interest calculator

The NASD also presents a comprehensive glossary of financial terms at:

www.nasd.com/Resources/Glossary/EntireGlossary/index.htm.

The SEC Web site also provides calculators, including: mutual-fund cost calculators, tax-free vs.

taxable yield comparison calculator, college savings calculator, loan calculator, savings calculator, mutual-fund breakpoint search tool, Social Security retirement planner, ballpark estimate retirement calculator, and 529 college savings plan expense calculator.

History hasn't proven that intelligence guarantees wealth. But by utilizing the above resources, perhaps we won't be the "fool and his money" that have been parted.

(November 2006)

FUN AND MONEY

With money in your pocket, you are wise, and you are handsome—and you sing well, too.

- Yiddish Proverb

Little-known facts about big money and holiday spending

At this time of year when excess spending is the norm, here are some monetary facts that might brighten your spirits, or at least enlighten you during those holiday spending sprees:

- How much cash is there in America? In November 2003, the "M1" money supply (which includes all coins, currency held by the public, traveler's checks, checking/savings account balances, NOW accounts, automatic transfer service accounts and balances in credit unions) was $1.25 trillion. That is on the order of $4,257 for each of us.

- The U.S. Secret Service was originated in 1865 to combat counterfeit money. There was a time when as much as one-third of all the money in America was counterfeit. The Secret Service estimates there is currently about $32 million of counterfeit currency in circulation in the United States.

- U.S. currency is not printed on paper, but on cloth: three-quarters cotton and one-quarter linen.

- A mile of pennies laid out is $844.80. By this standard, America is about $2.5 million wide from coast to coast.

- Parker Brothers has printed more money for its Monopoly games than the Federal Reserve has issued in real money.

- A check is merely an IOU, and IOUs can be written on anything. Someone once wrote a $15 check on an eggshell. The recipient took the eggshell to a bank in Canada, where it was cashed like any other check.

Spending average rises

According to one report, Americans spent an average of $1,395.06 per family on holiday gifts in 1984. Another report puts it at $5,580.25 per family in 1989 (The Wall Street Journal, December 1989).

In 2002, the American Sociological Review estimated that 4 percent of our annual income is spent on holiday presents. Median household income was $42,228 in 2001, according to the Census Bureau. That means holiday presents will cost an average of $1,689 per family. In New Jersey, the average is $67,914, yielding $2,717 in holiday presents.

Americans send 3 billion holiday cards a year. If you have the average number of friends, you should get at least 12 a year.

The average person spends 148 hours per year waiting in lines, more so in December than any other month. If you could be paid just minimum wage ($5.15 in Colorado) for those 3 1/2 work weeks, you would receive $762.20.

Your money and holiday shopping

Research has shown that music influences not only how much time people spend in a store, but also how much time they think they've spent in a store. It can even help promote one type of product.

A study in a British supermarket on how music could affect wine sales revealed that when the store played French music, people picked up more French wine. When the store played German music, Gewurztraminer sales rose.

The holiday shopping season offers innumerable examples of this kind of not-so-subtle musical message. It's almost impossible to go into a retailer in November or December and not hear carols designed to get us into the gift-buying mood.

Automated wallet may curb waste

Research affirms that individuals think about their purchases differently depending on whether they use cash, credit cards, debit cards, or checks.

They also put a much higher value on something they already own than on the same thing if offered for sale. This "prospect theory," which won the 2002 Nobel Prize for Professor Daniel Kahneman and cited his research partnership with the late Amos Tversky, helps explain why people hold on too long to losing stocks or pay way too much to insure themselves against small losses.

MIT Sloan School of Management Professor Dan Ariely and his graduate students are experimenting with an "electronic wallet" that would advise users on how best to spend their money. For example, your wallet may run a Monte Carlo simulation displaying how, based on your payment behavior, you would save $150 in the next three months by using cash for a purchase instead of your Visa card.

In other words, tomorrow's technologies will load the dice in favor of people not repeating the sort of silly statistical mistakes that lead to Nobel Prize-winning research.

And that will merit a prize of its own.

(December 2003)

Love and money – St. Valentine vs. St. Matthew

For many, December is the month of St. Nicolas and February is the month of St. Valentine. In this month, many will spend either small or large amounts of money to further the cause of domestic tranquility and admiration.

According to the Greeting Card Association, an estimated one billion valentine cards are sent each year, making Valentine's Day the second largest card-sending holiday of the year; even though the holiday was removed from its originator's calendar in 1969. At $2.50 a card, the annual economic effect is $2.5 billion, not to mention the florists, chocolatiers and restaurateurs.

"Valentine's Day is going to be more important than ever for retailers and marketers, because many retailers experienced a somewhat disappointing Christmas 2004," says luxury marketing expert Pam Danziger, president of Unity Marketing.

The National Retailers Federation reports that in 2004 the average consumer spent $99.24 on Valentine's Day, up from $80.44 the year before. Following those same lines, the amount per person should be about $110 this year. That will make total Valentine's Day spending over the $13 billion.

However, do St. Valentine and St. Dollar go hand-in-hand? Or, is it the more proverbial inevitable combination of death and taxes? One clue might be that all three of the "Valentines" canonized by the church were martyred.

It is frequently said that the "love of money" is the root of all evil. More specifically, money is the root of all marital evil. Therefore, the estimated $13 billion spent on the "day of love" may be fertilizing disastrous discord.

To bring more focus to the potential frenzy, the Consumer Credit Counseling Services in Phoenix engaged a research firm to reveal critical trends behind expenditures in the name of love.

According to the survey, Republicans are the stingiest, Independents the most frivolous, men spend more than women do, and the older people get, the less they spend.

On average, men will spend $121 while women will spend $83. Those under 35 will outspend those over 55 by more than $88 ($157 versus $69). Those in the age group 35 to 54 will spend an average of $93.

The survey also found that Republicans are the cheapest when it comes to dishing out the cash for love, as they will spend an average of $68, while Democrats will spend $94 and those heart-throbbing Independents will shell out $102. The survey made no conclusions regarding the overall budget deficit and partisan Valentine's Day spending habits.

As we all know, the Internet continues to intrude into more and more areas of our lives. In fact, there is a movement to make Saint Isadore of Seville the patron saint of the Internet. Hallmark may have a new market for a complete line of St. Isadore's Day cards.

ComScore Networks, Inc. found that 24 percent of holiday-minded shoppers would be buying their gifts online, spending 49 percent more in the most popular categories than the year before.

Traffic measurements from Nielsen//NetRatings revealed a huge 291 percent increase over last year to gifts and flowers sites for the week ending February 8, 2004, attracting 2.7 million unique visitors. The traffic to online greeting card sites for the same time period rose to 5.8 million, compared to 3 million in 2003.

In 2004, Internet users also looked for love in the week prior to Valentine's Day. 3.8 million unique visitors went to a personals site, a 9 percent week-over-week increase. Traffic to Yahoo! Personals grew 55 percent to 817,000 unique visitors from work and 1.3 million visitors from home, jumping 19 percent, while Match.com grew 19 percent at work to 863,00 unique visitors and 5 percent at home to 993,000 visitors.

But, how does our $13 billion investment in love stack up against the other side? Here are the contrary Valentine statistics.

In 2003 the number of marriages was 2,187,000, that's $5,944 of Valentine spending per marriage. However, the divorce rate was approximately 50 percent, or 1,093,500. According to MaritalStatus.com, the average cost of attorney's fees for a divorce is between $15,000 and $20,000-- $21.8 billion annually in attorney's fees alone.

Based upon pure financial theory and loosely applied empirical connection, it appears that our $13 billion of February valentine spending is essentially generating an additional $9 billion in economic stimulation from divorce proceedings. On the other hand, if consumers wish to save the $14,056 difference between marriage and divorce, they may want to reconsider the cards, flowers, and candy.

In case you're wondering, the patron saint of finance is Matthew the Apostle. Given the above, maybe there should be a "St. Matthew's Day," It could be assigned to April 15th.

(February 2005)

The latest catch phrases put the fun in financing

Every industry develops a vernacular language, words and phrases that have special meaning within that community.

Even the stolid community of finance and banking has a number of "catch phrases."

The following are some of the less-reverent, but revealing phrases in use today. Slang terminology grows out of behavior. Are there some lessons in these buzz-words?

Air-Pocket Stock - When the price of a stock plunges unexpectedly, similar to an airplane when it hits an air pocket. This is almost always caused by shareholders selling because of unexpected bad news.

Back Up The Truck - A situation where a large buyer scoops up huge quantities of a stock. In other words, when somebody "likes a stock enough to back up the truck," they are very bullish on it.

Big Uglies - A term used to describe the old industrial companies in gritty industries like mining, steel, and oil. Big uglies are often overlooked by investors seeking fast profits. Because of their bulletproof earnings, investors tend to flock to big uglies when the markets tumble.

Boomernomics - An investing strategy that involves buying equities directly related to Baby Boomers (people born between 1946 and 1964). Areas such as Biotech (youthful appearance), health care (longer life), and luxury cars (stylish rides) are sectors that stand to benefit from this theory.

Cockroach Theory - A market theory that states bad news tends to be released in bunches. Why the name cockroach? It's because cockroaches tend to travel in large groups and aren't looked upon kindly.

Cookie Jar Accounting - An accounting practice where a company uses generous reserves from good years against losses that might be incurred in bad years. This creates "income smoothing," because earnings are understated in good years and overstated in bad years. When companies take special charges or write downs, that's another flavor of cookie jar accounting.

Dead Cat Bounce - A temporary recovery by a market after a prolonged decline or bear market. In most cases the recovery is momentary and the market will continue to fall. Remember the saying: "Even a dead cat will bounce if dropped from high enough!"

Eat Your Own Dog Food - An idiom referring to the action of companies using their own products for day-to-day operations. A company that eats its own dog food uses its own products. This slang was popularized during the dot-com craze when companies did not implement their own software and thus could not even "eat their own dog food."

Footsie - A slang term for the FTSE 100 index. The Footsie consists of 100 blue chip stocks that trade on the London Stock Exchange.

Gazump - When the price for real estate or land is raised to a higher price than was verbally agreed on before. Basically, raising the price just before the papers are signed and the deal is delivered.

Gazunder - When a buyer reduces his/her bid for property before the transaction is signed and delivered. If the real estate market is crashing, a buyer might offer less because he knows that the seller desperately wants to sell the property.

Iceberg Order - Multiple orders that have been divided from a large single order and placed by participants in the market. The purpose is to hide the actual order quantity. When large participants, need to buy and sell large amounts of securities for their portfolios, they can divide the order into smaller parts. This reduces the price deviations in a particular stock's supply and demand.

Leading Lipstick Indicator - Coined by Leonard Lauder (Chairman of Estee Lauder), it follows the idea that when a consumer feels less than confident about the future, she (or he) turns to less expensive indulgences such as lipsticks.

Therefore, lipstick sales tend to increase during times of economic uncertainty or a recession. Believe it or not, this theory has been quite a reliable signal of consumer attitudes over the years.

Poop and Scoop - A highly illegal practice occurring mainly on the Internet. A small group of informed people attempt to push down a stock by spreading false information and rumors (bashing).

If they are successful, then they can purchase the stock at bargain prices and quickly "dash" away. Bash and dash is the opposite of pump and dump.

David Berger, editor of **www.fool.co.uk**, said: "Jargon is an off-putting and an unnecessary barrier which serves only to protect the interests of the City's stockbrokers, fund managers and pension companies."

Now that you're armed with the latest in pecuniary lingo, you too can mingle with the moguls in confidence.

(June 2003)